HUBBLE
BUBBLE

HUBBLE BUBBLE

TITANIA'S BOOK OF MAGICAL FEASTS

TITANIA HARDIE

PHOTOGRAPHS BY SARA MORRIS

QUADRILLE PUBLISHING

This 'saucery' is not so much for, as inspired by, the wonderful people in my life who cook with the freshest ingredients, and the most generous and loving hearts:

First, the 'Pilton set' – Jenny, Gerrie (queen of puddings), Candace, and my Aussie neighbour and lamington specialist, Sally Goldie; the 'almost Pilton set' – Boots, P, Solange, Winkie and Don, and Ed and Jude Burns; the 'witty as well as ornamental' – Hamish, Pip, Lucille Hoose, Orlando Murrin, John Flynn, John Grant (oh John, those dinners and Debussy), Oleh, Marion Charlouis, my step-son Luke, my sister Wendy, my cousin Laurie, and my brother-in-law Michael Franck – never a dull moment, or a second-rate mouthful, at any of these establishments. But most importantly, this book is for and because of my father Peter Charell (still the best cook ever in my life, among a glittering gallery); my mum, Sam (who learned rather later in her life – but no one knew better how to cook love and magic into her dishes for her second partner, Ron); my Aunty Zena (who knew everything about puddings and baking); and my amazing, tolerant, kind-hearted, and utterly original husband Gavrik Losey – the serious chef in my life. For the years of magic – in the kitchen and beyond – I love you all.

ALONSO: What harmony is this? My good friends, hark!

GONZALO: Marvellous sweet music.

Enter several strange shapes, bringing in a banquet, and dance about it with gentle actions of salutations, and inviting the King etc. to eat, they depart.

SEBASTIAN: A living drollery! Now I will believe

That there are unicorns; that in Arabia

There is one tree, the phoenix throne, one phoenix

At this hour reigning there!

SHAKESPEARE, WITH HIS OWN STAGE DIRECTIONS, IN THE TEMPEST III,3.

Also by Titania Hardie

HOCUS POCUS: Titania's Book of Spells

BEWITCHED: Titania's Book of Love Spells

TITANIA'S ORAQLE: A Unique Way to Predict Your Future

TITANIA'S WISHING SPELLS: Health, Wealth, Love & Happiness

ENCHANTED: Titania's Book of White Magic

ZILLIONZ: Titania's Book of Numerology

TITANIA'S FORTUNE CARDS

WHITE MAGIC: Titania's Book of Favourite Spells

TITANIA'S SPELL CARDS: Love & Success, Health & Happiness

Introducing the art of culinary magic

"If music be the food of love, play on…"; "the way to a man's heart is through his stomach"; "better is a dinner of herbs where love be …"; "for he on honey-dew hath fed …". The connection between appetite and love or mood is well attested. Food has the task of nourishing the body and brain, love of feeding the soul and spirit, and sometimes the two overlap. The writer Isabel Allende says, quite simply, that any food prepared with love has magic in it. This, then, is our journey – to celebrate the link between physical sustenance and love: between the feeding of the body, and of the soul and heart. En route, magical things may happen. The time-honoured tradition of the romantic candlelit dinner for two takes on a new guise as we investigate the way in which to weave magic into meals, turning every recipe into a spell. Food acquires magical properties both in the way that it is handled, and in an understanding of the powerful properties that the ingredients themselves may contain and therefore the physical effects they may have. The landscape of culinary magic is made up of many traditional dishes, and some that are brand new. There are recipes in these pages that derive from a long tradition of Celtic feasts, when 'magical' ingredients were often slipped into dishes to encourage a euphoric mood among the celebrating participants. There are also many new arrivals – dishes that owe their lineage to the modern enthusiasm for trying new herbs and flowers in cookery, and to our brave new taste buds, which have become so sophisticated in barely a generation. There are so many ingredients now available that old-favourite herbs now compete with chic new additions that were once available only to those with a garden.

The power of magical thought

Aphrodisiacs have long had a place in our romantic imaginations, but is there any truth in their efficacy? Herbs, we know, add flavour and garnish to the dishes we eat; but what more can they do to affect our moods? Does the choice of a particular menu favour one situation rather than another. And, does even the time of year – working with all the elements of psychic thought – enhance the magical dimension of food for certain romantic situations? In the recipes ahead, we will taste with all of our senses in a heady state. We will mix herbs and spices with a knowledge of their medicinal properties, lay the table with an understanding of the influence of colours and scents, and cook up a storm of emotion as we knead, blend, stir, and shape our ingredients into a harmonious whole. This is a task for all chefs, whether male or female, younger or older, experienced or new to the art. If you undertake to cook the magical recipes in this book, you will be taking your approach to food in a new and exciting direction. The recipes are not difficult, but the whole enterprise will require from you a little faith and an attitude of easy playfulness, as well as a willingness to work with the ingredients, genuflecting to their individual energies and spirits. Use your heart to guide you and you will soon be able to make magical things happen at your table. ❥ AS THIS HAPPENS, OTHER UNEXPECTED BUT NEVERTHELESS ENCHANTING CHANGES WILL TAKE PLACE. For instance, you will find that food prepared with love and the focus of beneficent thought will turn out tasting better. Dishes will work well; nothing will seem too difficult. Cooking up your ingredients with a feeling for their magical potential will alter your awareness of the littlest things around you. The wholeness of approach and psychological state will become obvious in its importance, and will somehow become a way of life. Magic will be infused in your very touch, on all things.

Cooking with attitude ❥ THE IMPERATIVES IN YOUR APPROACH ARE ONLY

THREEFOLD. Firstly, undertake only to weave magic into your dishes where it is appropriate to do so. In other words, no seduction dinners if your prospective partner is still attached to someone else, and no conception puddings to aid fertility if your partner is not even prepared to consider the matter of adding to the family. Respect at all times that magic should not flatly contravene another person's free will. It should be an invitation to a new, happier plane – not the subliminal twisting of a deeply unwilling arm. ❥ SECONDLY, ENJOY EVERYTHING YOU DO IN THE PAGES AHEAD. If you are tired or pushed for time, choose a very simple menu, and give its few steps of preparation all your love instead of all your time. Your attitude is everything. With the right psychological expectations and hopes, you will work magic into your food with ease, turning plain bread and soup into a feast for the gods. Even the place settings and choice of music can also create a large part of the magical effect you seek: so relax, and do this all in your easy stride. ❥ THIRDLY, BE BRAVE ENOUGH TO TRY ANYTHING IN YOUR COOKING. Don't feel that any recipe is beyond your talent, and don't be timorous when you set out on something new. Confidence leads to success, and I believe the mind arranges what will happen by the very positivity of its approach. If you see, in your mind's eye, a successful and beautiful dish as the outcome, so shall it be! This is true of any recipe you try, for any occasion, but it is especially helpful if you are whisking up something special for a lover. Confidence in your cookery will blend into an overall confidence in your body language and manner – which spells 'success' in love!

Recipes for every occasion

THE RECIPES THAT FOLLOW ARE BY NO MEANS ALL DEDICATED TO ROMANCE. Many of the chapters work around the idea that magic is to be shared with family and friends. You can weave a charm around your guests at a summer picnic or at the Christmas table. You will soon gain a reputation for unmatched culinary skills, and your individual beloved or gaggles of guests will fall under your spell of delight. Hospitality has such a potential charm, and you will have magical powers with which to make the most of this. REMEMBER THAT, WITH FOOD, THE SIMPLEST GESTURES GO A LONG WAY. You may be worrying about having enough time after a long day's work to make a really magical meal, or investing such a lot of energy in a whole menu. Though the recipes are chosen within each chapter as a themed menu, you can take any one dish and add it to an everyday meal if time precludes your throwing several courses together. Or, if you're the kind of cook who buys ready-made meals for convenience and time, take some ideas from the recipes here to add a few more exciting ingredients to them: add lavender buds to ready-prepared chicken, or a few saffron strands forked through your microwaved rice. THE FINAL RECIPE IN EACH CHAPTER IS DESIGNED AS AN EDIBLE TAKE-HOME GIFT FOR YOUR GUEST. If you're paying a visit to someone special, you might like to choose one of these items to make and take. Or just bake a simple cake, cover it with whipped cream, and strew the top with pretty rose petals, violets, orange-blossom, or any other scented flower. By this means you can carry a little magic into any situation – even the office picnic. Make a wish as you cut the cake with friends or a lover, and believe in the power of this thought to bring the wish home and true.

Creating a magical setting

YOU NEED FEW SPECIAL TOOLS TO CREATE MAGIC IN YOUR COOKERY. Candles of various colours have an important function at your dinner table, just as they do in ritual magic. Scented candles or fragrant oils in burners can have a bearing on the mood of your guest(s), amorous or otherwise. Music adds another ingredient, just as important as the herbs or the wine. A little knowledge can be employed to brilliant effect. IN EACH CHAPTER WE PREPARE FOR THE FEAST AHEAD WITH APT TABLE SETTINGS AND DECIDE ON THE APPROPRIATE COLOUR SCHEMES. Whether you are cooking for someone with whom you already live, or for friends who often come round, the variation in colour approach will always take them by surprise and prevent that feeling of complaisance. This doesn't mean you have to lash out a fortune on different sets of china in rainbow colours: but do have some serving bowls, place mats, or table coverings that can accentuate different elements in your china pattern, and extend this with, perhaps, one dominant colour in flower posies. Or, if you are just getting started with entertaining, choose something in a neutral colour which can then be played with in several ways. My first set of crockery was made of glass, so that every day I could place flowers, or mats, or coloured cards and napkins around and under them to change their appearance. A few rearrangements like this can alter the feel of a whole table: switching the colour scheme of your table from powdery blue or lavender to vibrant reds or fuchsia pinks moves an atmosphere of relaxation to one of passion at a stroke. Once you get into your stride, there is nothing to stop you even doing this between courses. ❦ NEVER UNDERESTIMATE THE IMPACT OF HAVING TAKEN A LITTLE TROUBLE. Guests always seem to notice tiny, unusual touches – and it will noticeably heighten their receptivity. Unexpected ingredients, unconventional colours and magical olfactory delights will remind those for whom you are cooking of your special and original personality – and, in turn, it will make them feel more special. Nothing could be more magical.

Irresistible invitations ❦ HERE ARE A FEW IDEAS FOR SPICING UP ANY SUPPER OR

LUNCH INVITATION: ❦ GIVE EVEN YOUR CLOSEST FRIEND A PROPER HAND-WRITTEN INVITATION, perhaps delivering it with a balloon or a flower, or tie the invitation with ribbon to a home-made biscuit with the centre punched through, or tuck it into the edge of a pretty potted herb. For a really special occasion, give a child some pocket money to dress up in a fairy (or other appropriate) outfit, then drive them around to hand-deliver the invitations. Alternatively, if you have a canine friend who won't eat the important information, pop a scroll into his or her mouth and let your friends laugh when they answer the door bell to this unusual footman. If your invitation style is usually by e-mail, send the message along with an on-line greetings card to raise a smile at the other end. ❦ FOR EVEN THE MOST LOW-KEY DINNER OR LUNCH GATHERING, make a small wreath of fresh seasonal flowers to announce your pleasure at the company of these friends at your door. They will feel as though it is Christmas all year round, and your artistic touch will grow with every attempt. You will find it enhances your own pleasure too, as well as being a way of properly observing the season. ❦ ASK YOUR FRIENDS TO DRESS IN A COLOURED THEME OR A MOOD. A 'red' dinner, or a 'sixties' lunch, or a 'seaside' barbecue, will put them in sparkling spirits before they even arrive at your door.

A spell for laughter and joy ❧ Do a short ritual before guests

ARRIVE: light a simple candle of your choice of colour, imagine the light from the flame filling the dining area, and hear in your inner ear the sounds of laughter warming the room. If you are hoping the meal will be romantic, scent the air with rose oil as you do the spell, and choose a pink candle for gentle love; make it a lavender candle with lavender oil for a bit of sensuality, and a white one spiked with jasmine or tuberose oil for high-voltage passion.

Make every meal a magical experience ❧ I hope

THE WHOLE SPIRIT OF THE BOOK WILL HELP TO DEMONSTRATE THE NEED FOR SHOWING A BIT OF FESTIVE SPIRIT IN EVERYDAY SITUATIONS, or how to capture that special feeling of festivity in an ordinary meal. It will hopefully also encourage you to make stronger magic for any celebratory occasion. It is good to be reminded of the need for enthusiasm in our lives: the gesture of hospitality spreads wonderful warmth and happiness. It also helps us as individuals – along with our dearest friends – to remember the importance of balancing duty and the responsibility of work with outright merriment and release of pressure. Which leads to an important final idea… ❧ THE LAST WORD OF ADVICE IS OBVIOUS, BUT WARRANTS REPEATING. Enjoy everything you do towards your meal. Choose a menu you feel confident about cooking; take time beforehand and experiment a little with some of the recipes if you like. Allow yourself time to plan, and cook, and still have time to get ready yourself. And, don't panic – food tastes better and exudes an enchantment if it looks as though you're completely in control. For the first-time cook this may seem impossible at first, but practice makes perfect. I like chef John Torode's philosophy, echoed in the title of his book: *Relax, it's only food.* ❧ AS WITH ALL OTHER ASPECTS OF MAGICAL PRACTICE, enchanted food is an extension of your own magical thought. The cornerstone of this concept is that you can manifest everything through powerful, concentrated thought. Translate this as positive thinking, or visualisation; your food becomes the medium through which your magical thoughts reach others. Therefore, returning to Isabel Allende, prepare everything (and that includes the sandwich you take to work) with love and bonhomie. It will bounce back on you, and sweeten the lives of everyone you touch. Lace the world around you with magic. ❧ BON APPETIT.

ATTRACTION

A MOROCCAN FEAST

THE MENU (SERVES 4-5) ☙ Salad of

warm goat's cheese ☙ Moroccan chicken

☙ Couscous with almonds and apricots

☙ Upside-down pear and ginger cake ☙

Home-made chocolate terrine

As we approach the Spring Equinox, we become more alive to our senses; and harnessing this renewed sensuality triggers attraction. Whether we are dusting off the winter lethargy from an existing love affair or putting out glowing signals for a new love, this is the moment to invite attention romantically. And what better way than to invite three or four friends around to share a spicy repast while you flirtatiously cook your way into someone special's affections…

Seductive spice mix

◗ OUR MAGICAL JOURNEY BEGINS BY FOLLOWING THE SPICE ROUTE TO A MOROCCAN FEAST. The exotic fruits of the Spice Islands have an attraction all of their own, creating a magical effect in food and warming up our senses. This easy menu centres on spice so that the witchy properties work from first to last in the food itself, but leave you free of fuss to enjoy your own party. ◗ CINNAMON IS A MALE APHRODISIAC; ginger's amazing digestive properties help to calm those butterfly tummies, so you can exude easygoing charm to the one you fancy; cardamom and cloves give off warm enticing aromas and also counteract the garlic, to leave your breath sweet for a lingering good-bye kiss! ◗ BEGIN WEAVING THE MAGIC INTO YOUR COOKERY BY CHOOSING AND BLENDING YOUR SPICES WITH LOVE AND GREAT CARE. It may help you into a bewitching frame of mind if you start with a journey to a market or specialist shop to buy your spices, just to give them a more ceremonial feel. Set aside a small, pretty bowl to blend them in: this is where the magic begins to brew, so make your spice mix the night before. ◗ FIRST, PURIFY YOUR HANDS WITH A LITTLE ROSE OIL AND, as you rub it in, make a little wish for success in both the cooking of the meal and the gift of good feeling among your friends – especially one! After this, you should blend your spices, whispering warm incantations and wishes over them as you mix them.

YOU WILL NEED

3 teaspoons ground cumin ◗ *2 teaspoons ground cinnamon* ◗ *2 teaspoons paprika* ◗ *½ teaspoon cayenne* ◗ *1 teaspoon ground coriander* ◗ *1 teaspoon saffron powder* ◗ *a few saffron strands* ◗ *½ teaspoon ground cloves* ◗ *2 teaspoons ground ginger* ◗ *3 teaspoons salt*

◗ BLEND THE SPICES IN THE BOWL WITH YOUR FINGERS, THINKING ONLY THE MOST POSITIVE THOUGHTS AS YOU WORK. See warmth growing between you and your special guest, and indeed a bonhomie encircling everyone at your table. Finish by covering the dish with a silken cloth, leaving the flavours and the magic to steep together overnight.

Scenes from Arabian nights

"IN MOROCCO", SAYS AN OLD PROVERB, "YOU MAY EAT WITH YOUR EYES". The visual element is a vital component, and hospitality is a sacred tradition in Islamic culture. Spare no energy in weaving your magic.

The Moroccan colour palette

THE COLOURS OF ATTRACTION ARE TRADITIONALLY FROM THE FLAME PALETTE: BUT LOVE ALSO VIBRATES ON PINKS. Draw inspiration from either or both of these hues to set everyone's pulses racing and celebrate the waxing light of spring and love. THESE COLOURS ALSO BELONG TO THE SPICY MOROCCAN THEME, AND WILL LEND A WONDERFUL EXOTIC FEEL TO YOUR TABLE. SWATHE THE TABLE WITH LAYERS OF SILKS: swag different shades of red and pink around the chairs, or borrow a few scatter cushions from friends to seat guests on the floor and eat around a low table. Invite them to kick off their outdoor shoes and put on a pair of Moroccan slippers to alter their mood. Garnish the room with simple, clear-coloured bowls of mauves and reds, or greens and blues, bearing figs, or bold chillies and red peppers, or olives and lemon wedges, or apricots and nuts. Place slices of Turkish delight in silver dishes or shells.

Sensual scents and sounds

DON'T FORGET THE SCENT OF YOUR ROOM: FOR LOVE, THE SMELLS OF COOKING ARE NOT ALWAYS ENOUGH. The Moroccan spice mixture *ras el hanout* is renowned as a potent aphrodisiac: you can enjoy playing on the principal scents from its more than twenty ingredients. Use a burner or some incense to fill the warm air with cinnamon, rose otto and woody essential oils; or blend a proper pot pourri focusing on rosebuds, cinnamon sticks, ginger pieces and cumin seeds. The effect of these heady scents will have the double advantage of sending your other guests home early to enjoy the mood created for them, and giving you a little private time with that one special person at your table.

MUSICALLY, PREPARE YOUR FRIENDS FOR A SPECIAL OCCASION BY FINDING SOMETHING WITH A MOORISH FLAVOUR.

The tea glass

THE ESSENTIAL INGREDIENT OF THE MOROCCAN TABLE IS THE TEA GLASS, WHICH COMES IN A VARIETY OF COLOURS AND PRICES FOR ALL BUDGETS. They look deliciously inviting as a centrepiece filled with sweets or chocolates, and festooned with pearls and other jewels. Your guests will feel inspired to undo their own top buttons and live a little dangerously, while magically, the glass embodies the spirit of fire, and pearls the spirit of water – the two key elements for passion and emotion. If you can't achieve the pearls, the elemental magic is still achieved once the glasses are filled with wine or water. DON'T FORGET THE FLOWERS, TOO. These could be tied into pretty spring posies incorporating your colour theme, hung from the corner of each chair, or placed in front of each table setting with a guest's name tied into each with a label. Try to include a crocus, the giver of saffron, for a magical connection.

A spell for the success of your entertainment

LIGHT TWO LARGE CANDLES (PILLAR CANDLES ARE BEST) – perhaps one in fuchsia pink and one scarlet red – just before your guests arrive, and make a short magic spell using them. Carefully word a brief appeal to the god of love for a successful evening, and invite your special friend to see you in a vibrant light. Then quickly imagine the rosy-pink light encircling the room and creating an atmosphere for love which will entice merriment and delight from every face at your table.

Dressing up

LASTLY, YOUR OWN PREPARATION: REMEMBER TO DRESS FROM THE UNDERNEATH OUTWARDS. This may seem obvious, but choose your flame/pink colours from your underwear up. Anoint your temples and body with a little rose oil for purification and, vitally, love. The rose will also blend beautifully with the smells emanating from your kitchen. Choose clothes that are tactile: in witchcraft, attraction starts with touch. Silks are perfect for this, whatever your gender. To add to the joy, ask your guests to wear something silken too: it will introduce anticipation of mysteries to unfold.

Salad of warm goat's cheese

THIS IS A LIGHT STARTER WHICH WON'T DEPLETE THE APPETITE BEFORE THE COUSCOUS. The combination of goat's cheese and salsa has a heady effect.

YOU WILL NEED

4 thick slices (about 1 cm/½ in each) goat's cheese • a little olive oil • 2 garlic cloves, sliced • 2 sprigs fresh rosemary, destalked • a large bunch rocket

FOR THE SALSA: 1 large onion, finely chopped • 2 tablespoons olive oil • 2 red chillies, deseeded and finely chopped • 1 large orange or yellow pepper, deseeded and thinly sliced • 1 x 400g/14 oz tin chopped tomatoes • 1 small bunch of coriander, roughly chopped • 1 or 2 kaffir lime leaves

MARINATE THE CHEESE SLICES in a little olive oil with the garlic and rosemary for a few hours or, preferably, overnight.

TO MAKE THE SALSA: lightly sauté the onion in the olive oil until translucent. Add the chillies and stir for a few minutes. Add the peppers and cook for a few minutes until soft, then add the tomatoes. Simmer over a very low heat for about 30 minutes, then add the coriander followed by the lime leaves, torn very loosely into the mixture. Cook for a further 5 minutes.

TO ASSEMBLE THE DISH, make a bed of rocket leaves, place a slice of cheese on top, drizzle any remaining marinade and then trickle the salsa over the cheese. Serve at once.

Moroccan chicken ❧ THE CHICKEN WILL TASTE BETTER IF YOU RUB IT WITH THE OIL

AND GARLIC, then cover it with your previously prepared spice mix and set aside to steep for a good hour before you cook.

YOU WILL NEED

1 medium corn-fed free-range chicken ❧ *2-3 garlic cloves, crushed* ❧ *100 ml/3½ fl oz lemon juice* ❧ *100 ml/3½ fl oz olive oil* ❧ *the spice mixture from page 14* ❧ *2 lemons, quartered*

❧ IN A BOWL, RUB THE CHICKEN ALL OVER WITH A MIXTURE OF THE CRUSHED GARLIC, LEMON JUICE AND OLIVE OIL, THEN SPRINKLE OVER THE SPICE MIXTURE. Place in a baking dish and set aside for about an hour to allow the flavours to develop. Reserve the residue of the garlic, lemon juice and olive oil marinade. ❧ PREHEAT THE OVEN TO 200°C/400°F/GAS 6. Stuff the quartered lemons into the cavity of the chicken. Pour the residue of the marinade around the chicken, but not over it to avoid disturbing the spice mixture. Make a tent of foil around the chicken to allow the liquid to steam into the meat while it roasts. Put the dish in the preheated oven and cook for about 45 minutes, removing the foil for the last 15 to allow the skin to brown nicely.

❧ REMOVE THE CHICKEN FROM THE OVEN, QUARTER AND ARRANGE ON TOP OF THE COUSCOUS. Deglaze the juices from the roasting pan with a little more chicken stock to make a sauce for the chicken. Circle the dish with white light in your mind: then serve, with the sauce in a bowl on the side.

Couscous with almonds and apricots ❧ THE GOLDEN

GRAIN, COUSCOUS, BELONGS TO THE AREA OF NORTH AFRICA BETWEEN THE MEDITERRANEAN AND THE SAHARA. It forms the basis for the highly ceremonial royal cooking of Morocco. Traditionally, it is lovingly prepared by sieving and drying a wheat flour paste, working the grains with the hands. Even if you're using the convenient instant variety of couscous which is now available, think of the tradition of love that is the parent of couscous-making, and envelope your couscous with these same romantic thoughts.

YOU WILL NEED

300 ml/ ½ pint chicken stock ❧ *a few strands of saffron* ❧ *250 g/9 oz instant couscous* ❧ *125 g/4½ oz almond flakes* ❧ *125 g/4½ oz pistachio nuts* ❧ *125 g/4½ oz cashew nuts* ❧ *60 g/2 oz sunflower seeds* ❧ *6-8 dried apricots, thinly sliced* ❧ *125 g/4½ oz dried mixed fruit, chopped into small pieces* ❧ *a little chopped fresh mint* ❧ *60 g/2 oz butter* ❧ *salt and pepper*

❧ BRING THE CHICKEN STOCK TO THE BOIL WITH THE SAFFRON STRANDS. Pour the couscous grains into a bowl and pour over the stock. Leave to stand in a warm place for about 10-15 minutes. Dry roast the nuts and seeds in the oven for a few minutes. Put all the nuts, seeds, dried fruit and the mint into the large dish from which you will serve the couscous. When the couscous is ready, put it on top of this mixture and fork the whole through. Season with salt and pepper and, if you desire, a knob or two of butter (this can make the grains sticky, so you may prefer not to use butter, as I do).

Upside-down pear and ginger cake ● MY GRANDMOTHER

BELIEVED IN THE EFFICACY OF GINGER AS A ROMANTIC INGREDIENT; its spicy warmth revives the senses. This dish is not too heavy and perfectly follows the spicy couscous. I make this cake before starting the rest of the meal and set it aside in a warmish place for an hour or more, covered with a tea towel to keep it moist and warm.

YOU WILL NEED

60 g/2 oz butter ● 100 g/3½ oz light brown sugar ● 1 small tin of pear halves or quarters, drained ● 2 tablespoons pecan or walnut halves ● 125 g/4½ oz plain flour ● ½ teaspoon baking powder ● a pinch of salt ● 2 teaspoons ground cinnamon ● 2 teaspoons ground ginger ● a pinch of freshly grated nutmeg ● a pinch of ground cloves ● 1 large egg, beaten lightly ● 125 g/4½ oz light brown sugar ● 75 g/2¾ oz treacle ● 60 g/2 oz butter, melted, plus more for greasing the cake tin ● 125 ml/4 fl oz milk ● 2 tablespoons almond flakes, roasted, for decoration ● crème fraîche or ice-cream, to serve

● PREHEAT THE OVEN TO 180°C/350°F/GAS 4. Melt the butter and brown sugar in a saucepan until they combine smoothly. Pour this mixture into a well-greased, 20 cm/8 in cake tin. Place the pear segments in the tin, flat side down. Scatter the pecan or walnut halves around the pear pieces. ● SIFT TOGETHER THE FLOUR, BAKING POWDER, SALT AND SPICES INTO A LARGE BOWL. In another bowl, lightly mix the beaten egg, sugar, treacle, butter and milk. Combine the wet and dry ingredients and beat until the mixture is smooth. ● POUR THIS BATTER OVER THE PEAR AND SUGAR MIXTURE IN THE TIN AND BAKE IN THE PREHEATED OVEN FOR ABOUT 45 MINUTES. Let the cake cool in the tin a little before turning it out. ● SERVE IT WITH THE LIGHTLY ROASTED ALMOND FLAKES SCATTERED ON TOP, with crème fraîche or ice-cream for accompaniment. ● For a real Moroccan touch, serve this pudding accompanied by fresh mint tea in Moroccan tea glasses. Warm the glasses, then at the bottom of each put 1 teaspoon sugar and 2 teaspoons chopped fresh mint. Cover with boiling water and allow to stew for a few minutes. The mint revives the spirit and combats fatigue – a good thing at the end of a meal. It also freshens the breath, of course…

Home-made chocolate terrine ● DON'T BREAK THE SPELL OF YOUR

GUESTS' FEELINGS OF REVERIE AND JOY. Send them away with something to remember the night – and let your magic work on beyond the supper table. This easy recipe can be made a day or two ahead for convenience and added flavour. Buy some cellophane paper to wrap your edible gift.

YOU WILL NEED

250 g/9 oz dark chocolate (the best you can afford – at least 70% cocoa solids) ● *60 g/2 oz pistachio nuts* ● *60 g/2 oz pecan nuts* ● *60 g/2 oz Brazil nuts* ● *60 g/2 oz hazelnuts* ● *60 g/2 oz candied apricots* ● *60 g/2 oz candied orange segments* ● *185 g/6½ oz tin of condensed milk* ● *1 tablespoon Grand Marnier*

● ROUGHLY CHOP THE NUTS AND THINLY SLICE THE FRUIT. Melt the chocolate in the microwave, or a bain-marie, very slowly, chanting of love as you work. Add all the other ingredients, with the alcohol last, and combine carefully. ● PUT THE CHOCOLATE MIXTURE INTO A FOIL-LINED LOAF TIN, SMOOTHING THE TOP TO GIVE A FLAT SURFACE. Cover with cling film and chill for at least 6 hours. The flavour will improve over a day or two. ● WHEN YOU ARE READY TO SERVE OR WRAP IT, TURN OUT THE CHOCOLATE TERRINE AND CUT INTO THIN SLICES WITH A SHARP, HEAVY KNIFE. Wrap the slices in the cellophane to make little bags. Trim with a few rosebuds and ribbon – pink of course! ● THE MAGIC HAS BEGUN...

SEDUCTION
A SEAFOOD DINNER

THE MENU (SERVES 2 OF COURSE)

- Aubergine confit with pitta bread

- Thai king prawns with chilli and ginger

- Coconut ice-cream Figs

poached in Shiraz

Our appetite for love was whetted by the first stirrings of spring; but now we arrive at May 1, the riper spirit of spring on the edge of the hotter days of an awakening summer. This time of the year traditionally saw a celebration of fertility, as the earth was green and fecund, and the air balmier. This is the moment for true seduction — a romantic dinner celebrating outright sensuality. Metaphorically, this feast, with its aphrodisiac qualities, is designed to bring on a relationship to a physical union — or to remind an on-going one about the joys of physical intimacy.

Seductive flavours 🍎 The list of aphrodisiac properties of foods from all

COUNTRIES IS ENDLESS — AND PERHAPS LARGELY MYTHIC. Seafood, however, does contain zinc, which steps up the libido, so oysters may not be so over-rated. And when saffron lends its regal golden colour to the king prawns, it also lends a sensual quality. A paste of saffron anointed the bodies of Arab brides, and its aphrodisiac properties were harnessed — but some experts warn that too much saffron could have a narcotic effect, so respect the high price of the crocus stamen, and use it sparingly.

🍎 IN KEEPING WITH THE FRISKY NATURE OF THE MONTH OF MAY, THE FIRST COURSE OF YOUR MENU MUST BE EASILY PREPARED AND SENSUOUS TO EAT DRIPPING OFF THE FINGERS. As in the previous chapter, where our aim was to get things cooking between two attracted souls, the use of spices is to heat the blood a little, give courage, and lift the sharers out of the realm of the everyday. My Italian grandmother was a great believer in the powers of aubergine and the taste certainly persuades one's senses that warmer days are coming. Similarly, the dessert course is her home-made ice-cream, because the texture and taste famously inspire the senses, as ice-cream advertisements have wilfully promoted. 🍎 AS WITH THE PREVIOUS FEAST FROM MOROCCO, CARESS AND ENJOY ALL THE INGREDIENTS YOU WORK WITH. Select your produce from a market if possible or, if you buy from the supermarket in packets, bring them home and unwrap them from their plastic wrappings — free their spirits a little to release their magical properties. As you cook, sing a song of love and imagine success at every turn. Be exotic, and the erotic will follow. Remember that perhaps the greatest aphrodisiac is a large pinch of relaxed self-confidence carefully blended with a warm sense of humour. Leave any touchiness in your personality at the door and slip on a bewitching persona along with your apron.

Dressing the feast with a seaside theme

THIS IS THE TIME TO ARRANGE YOUR FOOD AND FORAYS TO A SEASIDE THEME. Water is the element that governs the sensual realm of the emotions, and the energy of the incoming tide has a hypnotic effect on our own body rhythms. Work around the notion of a picnic, or borrow a friend's house by the sea. IF YOU WISH TO PUT YOURSELF PROPERLY IN THE FRAME OF MIND FOR THIS, WALK ON THE SAND AND CARESS THE GRAINS: make wishes and inhale deeply, relaxing your soul and senses with the sounds and smells of the seashore. Work your magical thoughts in sync with this: vividly envisage the desired result of passionate consummation or rekindled physicality with the one you love. Use the smells and sounds to carry the power of your thought.

Mermaids in Manhattan

IF YOU HAVE TO SETTLE FOR A CEREBRAL TRIP TO SUCH A LOCATION, NEVER FEAR. Use your inventive powers and re-create the feeling of the sea in your own city-bound apartment, with a menu to evoke the moving tides of sensual human pleasures. There is a bright range of oceanic fragrances, and you could redecorate your bathroom or dining room with sea shells dripping with foody delights that make you and your dinner guest feel decadent. For the day or night of your seafood feast, grace shell-shaped dishes with herbed quail eggs; or place the salt and pepper in oyster shells. Drape strings of pearls around the edge of opaque plates, and give watery pastel colours the lead at your table – pale pinks and greens, blues and silvers – like shards of mother-of-pearl. Set beautiful candles in dishes of sand, and work on a blue/green palate to engender sensual emotions.

A scent of abandon

LAVENDER IS THROWING OUT NEW GROWTH AT THIS TIME OF YEAR, AND WILL FIT IN WITH YOUR COLOUR SCHEME WHILST STIRRING THE SENSES PASSIONATELY. Its connection with the blistering heat of summer in Provence, or hazy days in Italy, will blur the connection with the physical abandon and relaxation that accompanies hot weather. Strew white linen with this wonderful herb – dried or fresh – and set lavender oil burning in a different place from your oceanic smells to entice your partner to explore… Don't forget to perfume your underwear, and take trouble and time with every detail. It will affect your own playful mood, as well as your partner's.

Flower power 🍎 IN THE MIDST OF THIS ROMANTIC SCENE SETTING, DON'T BE AFRAID TO ADD

PLENTY OF VISUAL HUMOUR AND A SPLASH OF COLOUR. A few field or corn poppy flowers – free from any of the narcotic effects common to its relative, the opium poppy – will give a pulse of red to the blues, inviting passion, and stimulating your dinner companion's energies and amorous inclinations. One or two red poppies to garnish the plate will get you both in the mood for a flirtatious evening. And they're edible, too.

The siren's song: a note of enchantment 🍎 TAKE A

LEAF FROM THE BOOK OF THE FAMED SIRENS, those brilliant *femmes fatales* who lured sailors with their bewitching melody. 🍎 WEAVE A SPELL THAT EVEN ODYSSEUS COULD NOT RESIST: before your guest arrives, light a lavender or blue dinner candle and chant his or her name with gentle passion as you watch the flame kindle and dance. Ask for the perfect evening (or lunch/afternoon), and send rays of the candlelight spinning around the room to envelop the atmosphere with sensuality and warmth. Don't be too 'heavy' with your spell, or with your behaviour. Just exude sparkling confidence.

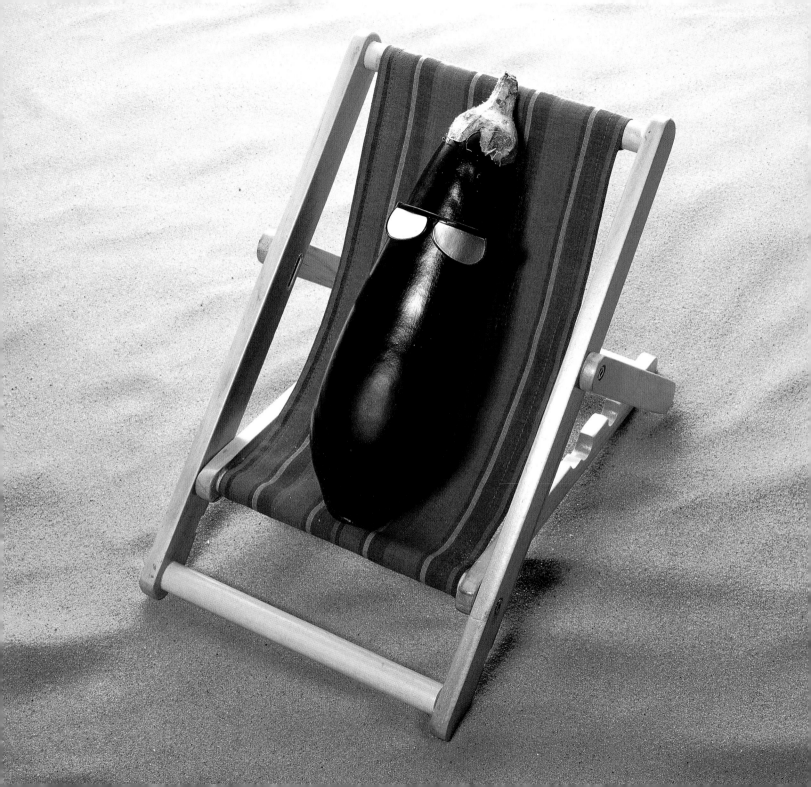

Aubergine confit with pitta bread

I HAVE CHOSEN THIS STARTER BECAUSE ITS FLAVOURS COMPLEMENT THOSE OF THE MAIN DISH, AND ALSO BECAUSE ITS SPICINESS STARTS THE GENTLE TASK OF PREPARING THE SENSES. Make this recipe a day ahead and store in the refrigerator, bringing it to room temperature before you serve with the warm bread. If you prefer, arrange it on a plate with a tablespoon of cottage cheese and a bit of salad – including the poppies.

YOU WILL NEED

1 large aubergine ● 2-3 tablespoons olive oil ● 2 garlic cloves ● 2-3 teaspoons lemon juice ● 1 teaspoon paprika ● pinch of cayenne pepper ● 1 teaspoon ground cumin ● a small bunch of coriander, roughly chopped ● salt and pepper ● warmed pitta bread or slices of cottage loaf, to serve

● PARE OFF STRIPS OF SKIN DOWN THE LENGTH OF THE AUBERGINE ABOUT 2 CM/³⁄₄ INCH WIDE AND 2 CM/³⁄₄ INCH APART, TO GIVE YOU A STRIPED EFFECT. Cut the aubergine across into slices about 2 cm/³⁄₄ inch thick, then place the slices on a large plate and salt them lightly. Set them aside for about 20 minutes, then turn them, salt the other sides and repeat the process. Rinse the aubergine slices well and dry on paper towels. ● PREHEAT THE OVEN TO 190°C/375°F/GAS 5. Brush a baking sheet with olive oil, then brush the aubergine slices very generously with the oil. Arrange them on the baking sheet and bake for about 30 minutes, turning them once during the baking. ● IN A BOWL, MASH THE BAKED AUBERGINE SLICES WITH THE GARLIC, HALF THE LEMON JUICE, THE PAPRIKA, CAYENNE, CUMIN AND SALT AND PEPPER TO TASTE. ● HEAT A LITTLE MORE OLIVE OIL IN A FRYING PAN AND SAUTÉ THE AUBERGINE OVER A GENTLE HEAT UNTIL ANY MOISTURE IS ABSORBED – this can take up to 25 minutes. Stir in the coriander and the remaining lemon juice. Serve with the warmed bread.

Thai king prawns with chilli and ginger ● THERE IS

SOMETHING IRRESISTIBLE ABOUT THE ALLURE OF SEAFOOD IN A SEDUCTION DINNER. Whether it is the sensual abandon of licking fingers, or just the idea of the extravagance of the ingredients, we are in the mood for love before we've tasted a bite. Add to this the belief in coriander as an aphrodisiac, and the capacity for both chilli and ginger to raise our internal temperature, and the stage is set for a dîner-à-deux to rival the famous scene in the film *Tom Jones*.

YOU WILL NEED

FOR THE DRESSING: *juice of 2 limes* ● *2 tablespoons palm sugar, or raw brown sugar if palm sugar is unavailable* ● *1 fresh red chilli, deseeded and finely chopped* ● *1 garlic clove* ● *100 ml/3½ fl oz coconut cream*

FOR THE SAFFRON RICE: *175 g/6 oz basmati rice* ● *1 teaspoon ground turmeric* ● *a few strands of saffron* ● *2 tablespoons desiccated coconut*

6 large raw king prawns in their shells ● *2 cloves garlic, crushed* ● *1 tablespoon grated fresh root ginger* ● *1 small fresh red chilli, deseeded and finely chopped* ● *2-3 kaffir lime leaves* ● *1 stalk of lemon grass, finely chopped* ● *2 tablespoons sunflower oil* ● *1 bunch of coriander, coarsely chopped* ● *1 bunch of mint, coarsely chopped*

● MAKE THE DRESSING BY MIXING ALL THE INGREDIENTS AND LEAVE TO STEEP. ● PREPARE THE SAFFRON RICE: MIX THE DRY RICE WITH THE TURMERIC, SAFFRON AND COCONUT. If you want to steam the rice, add 250 ml/9 fl oz of water to this mixture, then steam over boiling water for 20-25 minutes, stirring 2 or 3 times to ensure the saffron is mixed in. If preparing on the hob by the absorption method, put the mixture in a saucepan that has a tight-fitting lid, add 300 ml/½ pint boiling water and cook gently until all the water is absorbed and the rice is tender, about 15 minutes. Fork through once to fluff and separate grains. Keep warm. ● TOWARDS THE END OF THE RICE COOKING TIME, PEEL THE PRAWNS, LEAVING THEIR HEADS AND TAILS INTACT. Put the garlic, ginger, chilli, lime leaves and lemon grass into the oil and heat. When the oil is hot, add the prawns, and sauté very quickly, turning them once. Scatter over the chopped coriander and mint. Remove with a slotted spoon, place on a bed of saffron rice and pour over a little dressing. Serve with the remaining dressing in a bowl on the side.

Making Italian ice-cream ● MARCO POLO MADE A VITAL CONTRIBUTION TO

ITALIAN CUISINE WHEN HE BROUGHT MILK ICES BACK FROM THE EAST. This unsurpassable dessert gives every magic-making cook a chance to prepare something daringly different from store-bought ice-cream. Italian ice-cream is also unbelievably easy to make, as you don't need an ice-cream maker and there's nothing to do once the mixture is put in the freezer and you can prepare it any number of days before it is required. Once you have tried it, you will never want to eat any other ice-cream. If you have read *Like Water for Chocolate*, this is the equivalent opportunity in my family for working your tears and emotions lovingly into a dish.

Coconut ice-cream ● WE WILL USE THIS SEDUCTIVE COCONUT VARIATION TO

INTRODUCE THE ART OF MAKING ITALIAN ICE-CREAM. Make the ice-cream the day before your dinner. Serve with Figs poached in Shiraz wine (see page 39).

YOU WILL NEED

3 mixing bowls ● *4 eggs, separated* ● *200 g/7 oz caster sugar* ● *400 ml/14 fl oz double cream* ● *125 g/4½ oz packet of creamed coconut* ● *2 tablespoons Malibu, or other coconut liqueur*

● IN THE FIRST MIXING BOWL, BEAT THE EGG YOLKS WITH THE CASTER SUGAR UNTIL THE MIXTURE IS PALE AND FLUFFY. In the second bowl, whip the cream until it is thick but not solid: the cream will dictate the consistency of your ice-cream, so don't over-beat it. In the third bowl, whip the egg whites until they form stiff peaks. During all these processes, sing a song of seduction – your magical chant will be absorbed into the food as readily as into the air. ● NOW USE A LARGE METAL SPOON TO FOLD ALTERNATING SPOONFULS OF THE CREAM AND THE EGG WHITE INTO THE EGG YOLK MIXTURE. Incorporate plenty of air in your folding, as though you were making a soufflé. In between each addition, grate a little of the creamed coconut into the growing mixture, and keep on until all of the ingredients are combined – with a lightness of touch like a lover's caress. Finally, fold in the alcohol. (It is the addition of alcohol which is the secret of Italian ice-cream, as it magically prevents the ice-cream from forming ice crystals while it is freezing.) ● GREASE A PRETTY MOULD (like a small kugelhopf tin) and pour the mixture into it. Cover with cling film and freeze, undisturbed, for at least 8 hours and, better still, overnight. You do not need to take it out at intervals and whip the ingredients – it will form a perfect consistency if left entirely on its own.

Ice-cream variations

Flavour variations in this formula for ice-cream are as many as your imagination will allow, and every mood can find a corresponding flavour. Jasmine, gardenia and saffron are three of the more exotic, whilst chocolate and nut, or fresh strawberries, or vanilla and cinnamon, are all delicious – with sensual overtones. You will have an ice-cream 'spell' for any occasion. There is no better foody expression of your magic.

Saffron ice-cream with pistachios

Grind 4-5 cardamom pods (which also freshen the breath) and a few fennel seeds in a mortar with a pestle. Whip these into the cream some time before you beat the eggs, to give the flavours time to steep at room temperature. Then proceed, adding a small sachet of saffron threads to the egg yolks. At the point where you fold all the ingredients together, add the alcohol (sherry is a nice alternative) and about 60 g/2 oz of roughly chopped pistachio nuts. Cover with cling film and freeze as before.

Gardenia ice-cream

Lavender, or other strongly scented flowers like honeysuckle, sweet pea, violet or jasmine, could be used as flavourings in the same way. A few days before making the ice-cream, perfume the caster sugar in a tightly lidded jar with several scented gardenias or other flowers – make sure you begin with dry blooms. Shake them very gently each day to incorporate the scent. Beat the egg yolks with the perfumed sugar, and carry on without any other flavouring. When you reach the folding and the addition of alcohol, you could add a few petals of the flowers and a very plain alcohol, such as Kirsch or a splash of brandy. Don't use a heavy hand. Continue freezing as before and, when you turn out the ice-cream, garnish with a few of the flowers.

Strawberry ice-cream

Strawberries release endorphins in the system, making us feel good. Slice the strawberries and add (as you would have done the coconut) into the egg and cream mixture. Change the alcohol to kirsch.

Chocolate and nut ice-cream ❧ CHOCOLATE IS A WELL-KNOWN

APHRODISIAC, releasing a chemical whose effect is similar to the euphoric feeling of being in love. ❧ ADD A HANDFUL OF NUTS AND GRATED CHOCOLATE (as you would have done the coconut) to the egg and cream mixture. Change the alcohol to cognac.

Figs poached in Shiraz ❧ THE COMBINATION OF COCONUT ICE-CREAM AND FIGS

WITH SHIRAZ WILL LURE YOUR PARTNER ANYWHERE YOU WISH TO GO...

YOU WILL NEED

4 small ripe figs, or about 12 dried figs ❧ 2 cinnamon sticks (or 1 teaspoon ground cinnamon if not available) ❧ 250 g/9 oz caster sugar ❧ 300 ml/½ pint water ❧ ½ bottle (375 ml/13 fl oz) Shiraz red wine ❧ 1 teaspoon whole cloves ❧ 1 teaspoon whole black peppercorns ❧ 1 small sprig of rosemary ❧ 3-4 sprigs of young lavender plus lavender buds for decoration

❧ TO POACH THE FIGS, combine all the ingredients except the figs in a saucepan and cook, uncovered, stirring occasionally, for about 20 minutes, until the liquid has reduced by about a third and has thickened to a syrup. Add the figs and cook gently over a very low heat for about 5 minutes. Remove the pan from the heat and allow the figs to cool in the syrup. ❧ DIVIDE THE FIGS IN HALF AND SERVE EACH HALF ON A PLATE WITH A SLICE OF COCONUT ICE-CREAM. Spoon over the syrup and strew with lavender buds.

FRUITION

A SUMMER WEDDING BUFFET

The Menu (serves about 12) A celebration punch

 Salmon baked in a tent Lavender hollandaise Lavender

mayonnaise Rose sorbet Rose sweetmeats

If I were to choose the perfect date for a wedding, it would be June 21, the Summer Solstice, whichever hemisphere I lived in. This marks the celebration of the longest day and the beautiful, fecund earth. Here, clothed in all her glory, garnered with flowers and bathed in light, she shares her *joie de vivre* with her children. We all unwind, unbutton, unburden, smile more often in the full flowing summer. It is, quite literally, a magical moment and, when we're in tune with the earth's natural 'tides', everything we do seems to turn out better.

A celebration punch

MAGIC CAN BE ADDED TO EVERYTHING ON THIS BLISSFUL OCCASION, NOT JUST TO THE FOOD ITSELF. Introduce guests over a magical punch – a love potion gentle enough to let loose on the entire gathering to ensure that everyone gets on brilliantly.   IF YOU CAN FIND A COMMERCIALLY MADE ELDERFLOWER CHAMPAGNE, BY ALL MEANS USE THIS RATHER THAN ORDINARY CHAMPAGNE, AND OMIT THE ELDERFLOWERS. If you prefer a non-alcoholic version of the punch, substitute two large bottles of sparkling mineral water for the champagne. All the suggested flowers encourage the release of natural endorphins (feel-good chemicals) into the body, and taste delicious.

YOU WILL NEED

45 g/1½ oz fresh elderflowers if available, or 6-8 tablespoons elderflower cordial ● 2 bottles of dry champagne ● 2 small punnets of wild or alpine strawberries (the tinier the stronger) ● 1 tablespoon borage flowers (if unavailable, use small viola pansies or violets with 1 teaspoon borage tea)

● IF YOU ARE LUCKY ENOUGH TO HAVE FRESH ELDERFLOWERS, PICK THEM EARLY IN THE MORNING WHEN THEIR SCENT AND POTENCY ARE AT THEIR STRONGEST. Steep the flowers for about 1 hour in the champagne in a large jug in the refrigerator, covered with cling film (the champagne will go a little flat). Otherwise, use elderflower cordial.   REMOVE THE FLAVOURED WINE FROM THE FRIDGE AND STRAIN OUT THE FLOWERS. Halve the strawberries and some of the leaves to release their juices. Add the berries and leaves and a few borage flowers, or a little tea and/or a few pansy flowers or violets to the champagne mixture.   ALLOW TO STEEP FOR AN HOUR, then serve, if possible, with borage ice cubes.

Borage ice cubes

THROUGHOUT THE SUMMER, BORAGE PLANTS MAKE THEIR WONDERFUL, FRAGRANT, DELICIOUS BLUE STARFLOWERS. They are like little grains of fairy dust – brimming with a magical potency that can be harnessed to persuade your guests into soft and happy feelings.   HALF FILL EACH COMPARTMENT OF YOUR ICE CUBE TRAY WITH WATER AND FREEZE. Drop one or two flowers into each compartment, fill with water and freeze again. Borage ice cubes add a wonderful visual effect to a punch bowl and, as they thaw, the borage releases its powerful ingredients into the brew.

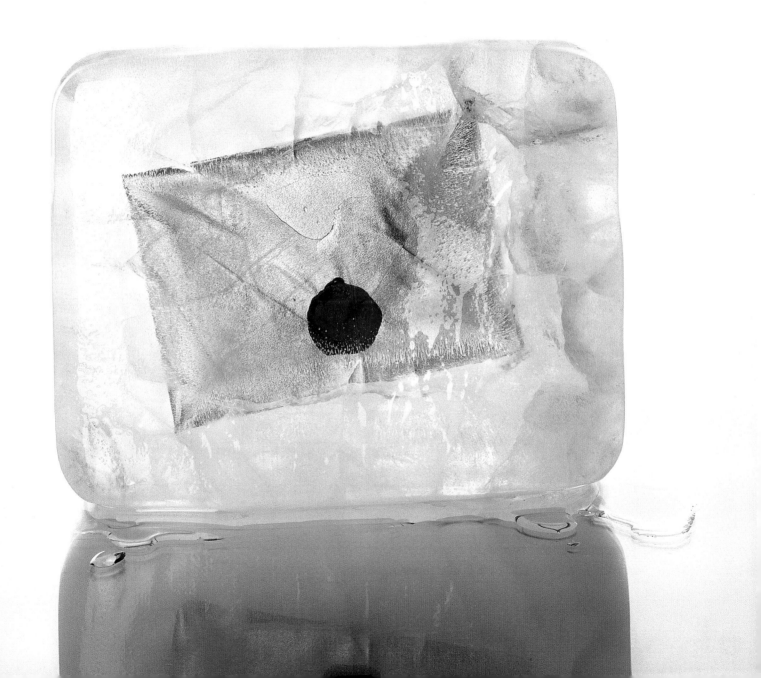

Setting the scene for love

THERE IS AN OLD SAYING, WHICH CAN BE TRACED EVEN TO CHAUCER'S WIFE OF BATH, THAT 'ONE WEDDING BEGETS ANOTHER'. Consider the probability that several single people, dressed in their best clothes and sweetest smiles, will come together and meet each other. Consider that the mood of a wedding is deliciously infectious, and that for at least that day, romance rules. These are ideal conditions for exuding love and attraction. ROSES ARE THE OUTRIGHT HARBINGERS OF LOVE. According to legend, the day Venus emerged from the sea a shower of full-blown flowers fanned her across the waters to her arrival at the shore. The scent of these queenly blooms has magical powers indeed – and we will ask them to be emissaries now to this theatre of love...

Rose-scented invitations

TO MAKE THESE YOURSELF, choose hand-made paper and scent it first by adding a few drops of rose oil to cotton wool and enclosing this, with some rosebuds or rose potpourri, in the box of stationery you are using. It will take about a fortnight to infuse the smells. INSCRIBE YOUR INVITATIONS WITH PERFUMED INK, by adding a few drops of rose oil to a small bottle of ink and allowing this to steep for a few days. Sprinkle rose petals or some rose potpourri into each envelope. Tie a rose-coloured ribbon, which has also been steeped in a little oil, round the envelope, then seal with a few drops of wax across both the ribbon and the join of the envelope, pressing a small rosebud into the seal as it hardens. This will immediately create an impact on the senses of your guests, generating anticipation of something magical to come.

Gilded place settings

LAY PLACE SETTINGS – whether informal and relaxed or more ordered and formal – that invite a complete surrender of the senses to the joy of the moment. IF YOUR WEDDING FEAST IS A BUFFET, it may be simple and informal, without a set place for all your guests, in which case, trim the buffet table as though it were the dinner table itself. Honour the goddess of love with a liberal bestowing of her sacred fruits. A pomegranate, if you can find one, looks sensational spray-painted in gold; but apples and pears are just as lovely, and will trip the senses into a new dimension. CHOOSE UNDER-RIPE FRUIT, and enlist a team of 'elves' or other summer sprites to help you paint them. A small piece of card, cut into a heart shape, or even a little luggage label, will look wonderful tied to the stem. Use your perfumed ink to write name tags for the guests, if they are to have places at the table, or for the dishes, if you are decorating the buffet table.

Wreaths of summer flowers

IF YOU ARE HOSTING THIS OCCASION AT HOME, make a welcoming fresh flower wreath for your door. A simple circlet of wire tied with roses and lavender, perhaps some honeysuckle or jasmine, and a few summer strawberries, will prepare your guests for the magic awaiting their palates.

CONTINUE THIS THEME WITH TINY POSIES FOR THE LADY GUESTS: make up small bunches, tie with ribbon, and secure a name card to the stems. This can be given as a parting gift, or used as place names for seating, and doubles as a beautiful floral touch on the most rustic of tables.

Silks and scents

DON'T LEAVE ALL THE CARE IN DRESSING TO THE BRIDE; from the underwear outwards, roses are your theme to promote a feeling of love among the guests. Orange flower (neroli) could be your choice if you want to be a little more eastern and exotic, for this is the sacred blossom for weddings in India and the East. Wash your lingerie in neroli or rose-scented liquid. Anoint your tummy button with a drop of rose oil or rose perfume, and tie a rose-pink ribbon around your middle for perfect love. Remember, you are venerating the earth's zenith of life, heat and light, so this can be your way of honouring nature. Do something special with flowers on your outfit, and consider that silk best expresses the floaty, hazy feel of summer.

The enchanted feast

WHEN PLANNING A WEDDING FEAST, consider that the food must be magical for everyone. The couple making their vows will need abundant perpetuation of their present happiness, while those who have helped at the wedding may be stressed, and need soothing. At a wedding, no note must be anything but sweet, and a few morsels of enchanted food can help to promote that bonhomie.

CHOOSE INGREDIENTS THAT SPREAD A FEELING OF EUPHORIA AMONGST THE GUESTS, such as borage, lavender, fresh mint, scented geranium, summer strawberry and pansy or violet flowers. Prepare food that can be made in advance. Take trouble about the details when you have the time to do so, then relax and let the guests and the feast itself generate its own magic.

Salmon baked in a tent ● Salmon is a versatile fish and can be cooked

in a variety of different ways. I have even heard of it being cooked in the bath, or in a dishwasher! Here, we will stick with a more traditional method.

You will need

1 large whole salmon ● a few large sprigs of fresh fennel ● 2 teaspoons mixed peppercorns ● 1 large lemon, sliced, and the juice from 1 more lemon ● a little sea salt ● 45 g/1½ oz butter ● 1 large glass of champagne or white wine ● lavender flowers, to decorate

● The best way to cook the salmon is to bake it in a tent of tin foil to steam the liquid flavours into the fish whilst retaining its moisture. Place the fish on a large foil-lined baking sheet or tray, and stuff the fennel, a few of the peppercorns and the lemon slices into the cavity. Rub the outside of the fish with a little sea salt and dot with one-third of the butter. Turn up the sides of the foil to make a boat, pour the champagne around the fish on the foil, and sprinkle over some more of the remaining peppercorns. Wrap the foil right over the salmon to form a tent and seal the sides. Bake for 35-40 minutes in a moderate oven. ● The fish can be served warm, first allowing it to rest for about 10 minutes after coming from the oven. Or, if you prefer to serve it cold, allow it to cool in its own juices, then transfer to a large plate. Skin, and decorate with lavender flowers. Serve with one of the sauces on pages 48-9. Accompanying vegetables could be baby carrots and fresh spring peas, or the Carrots with Almonds and Honey on page 106.

Adding saucery ❧ These sauces will lend the wedding feast much of its magic.

Choose according to preference, but the hollandaise is nice if the fish is to be served warm and the mayonnaise better if you are serving everything cold. ❧ Both sauces serve 6, so scale up as necessary.

Lavender hollandaise ❧ Don't be frightened about doing this sauce

properly: be confident, but keep a few drops of iced water beside you in case it threatens to separate. Work your loving magic over the brew, imagining light entering the sauce throughout the cooking process. The lavender creates a relaxed feeling of timelessness: no need to hurry the proceedings, just enjoy the ambience and culinary pleasure.

You will need

2 egg yolks ❧ *small squeeze of lemon juice* ❧ *175 g/6 oz butter, cut into small pieces* ❧ *3-4 drops of lavender oil* ❧ *salt and pepper* ❧ *a few lavender flowers, to decorate*

❧ In a small saucepan, beat the egg yolks with a whisk and add a few drops of lemon juice and water. As the sauce thickens, move it to the hob or a double-boiler and cook over a very low heat, whisking all the while: if the heat is too high, it will separate at once. ❧ Take the yolks almost to the point of scrambled egg but not quite, then add the first piece of butter away from heat. Whisk the butter into the yolks. Return the sauce to the heat and add another knob of butter, whisking the while. Once this has melted, incorporate another knob of butter (you might prefer to switch to a wooden spoon now). The mixture should become thick, but if the heat starts to separate the egg from the butter, take it off at once and add a few drops of iced water, stirring vigorously, until the mixture comes back. Continue adding all the butter – slowly, very slowly – until it is all incorporated. Then add just a few drops of lavender oil and a little salt/pepper to taste. Transfer to a sauce boat or bowl and serve.

Lavender mayonnaise ❧ THIS IS A VARIATION ON THE PREVIOUS SAUCE, and it could be appropriate to serve both, so your guests can choose which to have. The advantage of the mayonnaise is that it can, of course, be made a day or two before, whereas the hollandaise must be made just before the meal. Make sure that the eggs and oil are the same temperature before you begin.

YOU WILL NEED

1 egg yolk ❧ *½ teaspoon Dijon mustard* ❧ *salt and pepper* ❧ *200 ml/7 fl oz light olive oil (not extra virgin)* ❧ *1 teaspoon vinegar* ❧ *5 drops of lavender oil* ❧ *a little lemon juice (optional)* ❧ *2 teaspoons freshly chopped herbs (parsley or chervil is a wonderful complement to the lavender)*

❧ PLACE THE EGG YOLK AND MUSTARD IN A SMALL BOWL WITH A TOUCH OF SALT AND PEPPER, AND BEAT WITH A WHISK OR HAND-MIXER UNTIL VERY WELL BLENDED. Start to add the olive oil, at first only drop by drop, whisking continuously, until the mixture starts to thicken. Continue until you have used about half the oil. ❧ INFUSE THE VINEGAR WITH THE LAVENDER OIL AND STIR MOST OF THIS IN – the mixture will whiten. Now, continuing to whisk, add the remaining oil a tiny bit more quickly, in a continuous thin stream. Don't hurry, and make magical thoughts as you work, weaving a potion of love with which to bewitch all your guests... ❧ FINALLY, ADJUST THE SEASONING AND ADD THE CHOPPED HERBS, TOGETHER WITH EITHER A DROP OR TWO MORE LAVENDER-VINEGAR OR LEMON JUICE. This mayonnaise will keep in the fridge for several days in a tightly sealed jar and will improve in flavour.

Rose sorbet ❧

ROSES BELONG TO LOVERS AND ALSO HAVE DOZENS OF MEDICINAL, COSMETIC AND CULINARY PROPERTIES. The scent lifts the spirits and is used to cleanse and purify the environment. It also perfumes the body and freshens the breath. Here, used in a sorbet, it is an ideal celebratory ingredient for a summer wedding, symbolising the crowning of love. Pick the petals on a dry day when the roses are not fully blown; make the sorbet several days ahead to allow the flavour to develop.

YOU WILL NEED

2 large handfuls of highly scented rose petals (you will need 16-20 flowers) plus more to decorate ❧ 600 g/1¼ lb caster sugar ❧ 2 teaspoons rose water ❧ 3-4 teaspoons glycerine ❧ 2 egg whites

❧ PUT THE ROSE PETALS INTO A PAN WITH 350 ML/12 FL OZ WATER. Add the caster sugar and place over high enough heat to dissolve the sugar in the water, but not too rapidly. Allow the liquid to simmer very gently for about 20 minutes. Add the rose water, cover and allow to cool and stand overnight. ❧ THE FOLLOWING MORNING, STIR IN THE GLYCERINE AND – MAGICALLY – THE LIQUID TURNS PINK! Freeze the sorbet for an hour or two, until just beginning to set, then beat the egg whites to stiff peaks and fold in. Return to the freezer and leave until properly set: this will take several hours. Serve with rose petals or, for spectacular effect, in an open rose.

Edible gifts

IT IS TRADITIONAL FOR GUESTS TO TAKE AWAY WEDDING CAKE, but why not start a new tradition, borrowing inspiration from the Roman custom (still adopted by modern-day Italians) of silvered almonds. The idea is to bestow fertility, of which nuts were the symbol. Blend this with the medieval treats, or 'sweetmeats', and keep your roses blooming. Your magic will work on, long after the last guest has departed. STREW A FEW ROSE PETALS IN FLOWERY BOXES OR SMALL CELLOPHANE BAGS FOR GUESTS TO TAKE AWAY, and add some sweetmeats. Secure with ribbons anointed with rose oil, and hand-write the guests' names with an appended 'lucky wish spell'.

Rose sweetmeats

USE FRAGRANT ROSES – AN OLD VARIETY WOULD BE EXCELLENT, or a good new scented variety. Be sure that the roses have been grown organically, and that no pesticides or chemicals have been used on them.

YOU WILL NEED

200 g/7 oz flaked almonds, toasted • *4 tablespoons icing sugar, plus a little more for dusting* • *30 g/1 oz fresh deep pink or red rose petals (about 2 handfuls), plus a few more for decoration* • *225 g/8 oz caster sugar* • *2 tablespoons glycerine* • *1 tablespoon iced water* • *2 teaspoons rose water*

PULSE THE ALMONDS AND ICING SUGAR IN A FOOD PROCESSOR UNTIL WELL COMBINED, THEN ADD THE ROSE PETALS (MAKING SURE THEY ARE QUITE DRY). Process the mixture until the rose petals are finely chopped and the mixture looks pale pink. PUT THE CASTER SUGAR, GLYCERINE AND 2 TABLESPOONS OF WATER INTO A SAUCEPAN AND BRING TO THE BOIL, STIRRING, UNTIL THE SUGAR DISSOLVES. Continue boiling until the mixture is lightly caramelised– a tiny amount dropped into the iced water will make a soft bead. Remove from the heat and add to the rose and almond mixture in the food processor. NOW ADD THE ROSE WATER, AND COMBINE THE INGREDIENTS UNTIL A SMOOTH PASTE FORMS. Allow the mixture to cool completely, then knead it just long enough to make it supple. Roll the mixture into about 24 large or 36 little balls and dust with icing sugar.

FERTILITY
A MIDSUMMER BARBECUE

The Menu (serves four plus) 🍎 Lemon tuna or swordfish on skewers

🍎 Indonesian satay-style chicken kebabs 🍎 Lusty sauces 🍎 Barbecued

potatoes with basil butter 🍎 Lovers' salad 🍎 Summer fruit champagne jelly

This part of the calendar celebrates the period from mid-July (old St Swithin's day) through August with its Celtic festival of Lammas, the earliest summer harvest when the earth is golden ripe. Here we are in true summer time, with holidays and an atmosphere of *laissez faire*. The days – and nights – are heady and hot. We celebrate with a lusty outdoor feast cooked on an open fire – the barbecue – which, as well as being an Aussie institution, has roots stretching back to Celtic and Roman celebration. We needn't, however, go as far as spit-roasting a whole ox or pig: we'll keep this romantic and seductive…

In the mood for love ●

WE ALL FORGET TO SEDUCE OUR PARTNERS ONCE WE SETTLE INTO A ROUTINE. Whether we are with someone in a relationship of many weeks or many years, this chapter is dedicated to the vital task of creating a fantasy setting for adults. Simple, delicious food served in a verdant corner of the unhurried planet, or by a rhythmic seaside setting, is perhaps the best aphrodisiac in existence. We are all seduced by someone familiar taking a little trouble to create a small earthly paradise. ● OUR AIM IN THIS CHAPTER IS TO CREATE A FEAST FOR TWO OR TWENTY THAT ROUSES SENSUAL PLEASURES ON THESE HOT DAYS, WHEN TEMPERATURES – both seasonal and personal – rise. This is the moment of peak fertility, when the next spring will give birth to the creativity of this season. Nudge your partner into comfort and good humour: leave the mobile phone behind.

A spell to ensure fair weather ●

BEFORE YOU BEGIN, TRY A WEATHER SPELL TO ENSURE THE DAY ISN'T SPOILED BY RAIN (A REAL CHALLENGE FOR THOSE OF US LIVING IN THE BRITISH ISLES). Witches were long supposed to have powers over weather, and I have to say it worked for me on my daughter's name-day – the first hot, sunny day in July a few years ago, when we invited 60 people to eat in our garden. So see how good your visualising can be. ● TAKE A HANDFUL OF SAGE AND EARTH, TO CELEBRATE THE ELEMENT OF EARTH; some peppermint or spearmint leaves and a few flower petals to celebrate the elements of wind or air; Juniper berries and peppercorns to bring fire; and a little willow branch in a dish of water to invite this element. Mix these together, chant and envisage a beautiful day (or evening) on the date of your choice, dance a dance of reverie to the earth and heavens, and sprinkle the ingredients together around several trees or over flowers in a park or your garden. Boldly see a beautiful few hours to celebrate your outdoor fire-feast. Bow to the elements, and circle the vital day on your calendar. Imagine clear weather every day until the day... and good luck.

Setting the sylvan scene
You could be a forest god or goddess by arranging for your guests to arrive in a glade that is already mysteriously adorned with a trestle table laden with flowers and beautiful floral china. Add glasses, champagne cooling in natural water or a garden fountain, and perhaps even a block of dry ice, which exudes clouds of aesthetically uplifting vapours, and the atmosphere is set for spell-making. It would take a little planning, and perhaps a fairy accomplice or two, but the effect is literally enchanting.

Once you've decided on your location – and the degree to which the feast will be intimate or for many friends – you can prepare the terrain for love. Create a powerful atmosphere with outdoor lighting: beautiful garden flares, bowls bursting with petals and floating candles, or perfumed candles in outdoor lanterns, will release light and aroma to help to create a magical setting. Your smells cannot be light – for the air will disperse them. Choose strong scents that work outdoors, and kindle them everywhere. Lay down a rug and scatter herb pillows and cushions spiked with essential oils, so that sitting or leaning on them will release stirring floral scents. Both lavender and sweet peas will stand up very well to a light strewing across the blanket and release a powerful sensual aroma. If you're near a pine grove, tie little sprigs into muslin bags secured with ribbon, and place these under the cushions to release their scent as they're brushed and squashed. Pine soothes and revives sagging energy. If you want a colour theme, remember that purples and lavenders are the colours of passion and seduction, and pinks call up love. If the meal is just for the two of you, and privacy is not a problem, then perhaps outright red should be your colour choice. This is the colour of pure sex, and will increase the pulse rate by around 12% – but perhaps not an ideal choice on a day that is blisteringly hot. Lavender blues and greens, and soft mauves, will inspire passions while cooling the temples and inviting a shady togetherness. Don't forget music, for it will add the final note in the fairy setting. Of course you must choose something you (and your partner and friends) like, but make sure it fits into the setting. Heavy metal may not add much in a sylvan glade.

Sweet spells of love
To this magical location, add a splendid touch: write spells of love and passion on slips of paper, wrap them prettily in foil paper, and secure them with ribbons into the surrounding trees with a candle burning at the trunk below to release the thought. This is as charming in a public park – if a little less private – as it is in the woods or by the sea. Compose your spells of love, and let your imagination dance on fairy wings.

Glowing scented embers ● THIS IS A SUBJECT FOR A TINY GENDER DISCUSSION.

The male of the species seems to like the idea of doing fires for barbecues, but there's something divine about a lady taking charge of this masculine preserve. Don't be afraid of this. Remember, too, that the word 'perfume' reminds us that scent was originally released *par fume* – by smoke. This is therefore a delicious opportunity to seduce through the flames themselves. ● TO BEGIN WITH THE FUEL, ADD A LITTLE WOOD TO THE CHARCOAL. You need the intense heat of the latter to fire the food properly, but the wood will lend a delicious scent and flavour to the cuisine. Pine wood or chippings will add the delicious resinous smell of pine, as will juniper or cedar wood if you're lucky enough to have it. Otherwise, add herbs into the coals once they are glowing rather than flaming: rosemary and sage burn wonderfully, while bay adds magnificent flavour – but add it towards the end of the cooking process as it emits oils that can blacken the underside of the food. Lemon verbena, myrtle and thyme are also good choices, and citrus fruit peels will release their oil to add flavour and fragrance. If you can safely pick out one piece of glowing charcoal and set it to the side of the fire, tip some incense – such as benzoin or frankincense with a little sugar – on top to scent the air pungently with wild and wonderful imaginings.

● AND SO, TO THE FOOD...

Lemon tuna or swordfish on skewers

SERVE THESE SKEWERS WITH BARBECUED POTATOES AND LOVERS' SALAD (SEE PAGES 63-4). A SERIOUS FLAVOUR SENSATION CAN BE ADDED IF YOU USE THE STRONG, STRAIGHT STEMS OF WOODY HERBS – such as rosemary, thyme, lavender or bay – as the kebab sticks.

YOU WILL NEED

2 tuna or swordfish steaks ● *1 tablespoon soy sauce* ● *1 lemon, juice and rind* ● *1 lime, juice and rind* ● *small piece fresh ginger, grated* ● *1 small yellow and 1 orange pepper, deseeded and cut into chunks* ● *4 long woody herb 'skewers'* ● *8 garlic cloves*

● CUT THE FISH INTO PIECES (SLIGHTLY BIGGER THAN BITE-SIZED, TO AVOID THEM BREAKING UP). Mix the soy sauce, lemon and lime juice and the grated ginger in a bowl and marinate the fish in this for an hour or two, or overnight in the refrigerator. ● TO ASSEMBLE THE KEBABS: thread alternating pieces of the fish, chunks of differently coloured peppers and pieces of lime and lemon rind onto the herb 'skewers' (thyme is a good choice, as the meat is quite soft, and you can make a small hole through the vegetables with a regular skewer first). About every fourth item, also thread on a whole garlic clove.

● MARINATE WITH THE JUICES AND SOY UNTIL REQUIRED. Cook on the barbecue for 3-4 minutes, turning once and basting.

Indonesian satay-style chicken kebabs

YOU WILL NEED

2 large chicken breast fillets, skinned and cut into chunks ● *1 small onion, grated* ● *1 small piece of ginger, peeled and grated* ● *2 tablespoons brown sugar* ● *2 tablespoons soy sauce* ● *1 teaspoon mixed spice* ● *2 teaspoons peanut butter* ● *1 tablespoon groundnut oil* ● *1 green chilli, deseeded and chopped* ● *juice of 2 limes* ● *4 long bay, rosemary or lemon grass 'skewers'*

● PLACE THE CHICKEN PIECES IN A GOOD-SIZED BOWL. Combine all the other ingredients well, and pour this mixture over the chicken, tossing to coat well. Refrigerate overnight. ● PLACE THE MEAT ON HERB SKEWERS. Cook on the barbecue for 5-6 minutes, turning and marinating as often as possible. Serve with one of the lusty sauces on pages 62-63.

Lusty sauces

HERE IS A RAINBOW OF BRIGHT, FLAVOUR-PACKED SAUCES TO SERVE WITH YOUR FISH AND MEAT KEBABS. The ingredients were chosen for their aphrodisiac properties – all were tried and tested and passed with flying colours...

Basil cream sauce

THE MAGICAL PROPERTIES OF THIS BASIL CREAM WILL REKINDLE THE POWER OF LOVE.

YOU WILL NEED

2 spring onions, chopped ● *30 g/1 oz butter* ● *a few sprigs basil, coarsely chopped* ● *100 ml/3½ fl oz dry white wine* ● *250 ml/8 fl oz vegetable stock* ● *100 ml/3½ fl oz double cream*

● SOFTEN THE SPRING ONIONS IN THE BUTTER OVER LOW HEAT, then stir in the basil. Add the wine and reduce until almost all of it has evaporated. Add the stock, bring the mixture to the boil and simmer until the liquid reduces again by about half. Take off the heat, allow to cool a little, then whip in the cream. The sauce can be served warm or cold.

Champagne sauce

THIS IS THE MOST ROMANTIC SAUCE OF OUR TRIO.

YOU WILL NEED

1 small onion, thinly sliced ● *a little butter* ● *2 glasses of champagne* ● *300 ml/½ pint double cream* ● *salt and pepper*

● COOK THE ONION IN THE BUTTER OVER A LOW HEAT UNTIL TRANSLUCENT, then add the champagne and bring it gently to the boil. Simmer until the liquid reduces by about half, then add the cream over a very low heat. Simmer until the sauce reduces and thickens. If you want a smoother consistency, sieve it. Season with salt and pepper. Serve warm. This sauce is particularly good with fish skewers.

Tomato salsa 🍎 THIS SPICY SAUCE WILL TURN UP THE HEAT BETWEEN YOU. It has also been

discovered that tomato – especially cooked tomato – raises the sperm count...

YOU WILL NEED

1 kg/2¼ lb fresh tomatoes, peeled and roughly chopped, or 2 x 400 g/14 oz cans of tomatoes 🍎 1 tablespoon salt 🍎 ½ teaspoon cloves 🍎 ½ teaspoon allspice 🍎 2 teaspoons dry mustard 🍎 200 g/7 oz sugar 🍎 250 ml/9 fl oz white vinegar 🍎 4 red chillies, deseeded and chopped 🍎 2 green apples, finely chopped 🍎 2 onions, finely chopped 🍎 2 garlic cloves 🍎 1 teaspoon chilli purée or 2 teaspoons chilli sauce 🍎 2 tablespoons tomato purée

🍎 PUT THE TOMATOES IN A BOWL AND SPRINKLE WITH SALT, THEN SET ASIDE FOR AN HOUR. 🍎 COMBINE THE SPICES, MUSTARD AND SUGAR with the vinegar in a heavy saucepan over a medium heat and stir until the sugar dissolves. Bring to the boil, then add the remaining ingredients, stirring regularly. Simmer uncovered over a low heat for an hour, then pour into sterilised jars when cool. Seal and store. This salsa will develop in flavour nicely and is wonderful served with lamb or chicken.

Barbecued potatoes with basil butter

YOU WILL NEED

250 g/9 oz new potatoes 🍎 a few sprigs of fresh basil, chopped 🍎 1 garlic clove, crushed 🍎 200 g/7 oz soft butter 🍎 salt and pepper

🍎 SEVERAL DAYS AHEAD OF TIME, make the basil butter: put the basil, crushed garlic, butter, salt and pepper in a small dish and, using a heavy fork, mash the ingredients together. Cover with foil and then let the butter develop its full flavour for a few days in the refrigerator. 🍎 JUST BEFORE THE BARBECUE, remove the basil butter from the fridge to allow it to soften slightly. Parboil the potatoes. Drain and place in nests of foil (3-4 potatoes in each nest) on the barbecue. Allow them about 15 minutes to cook alongside your skewers. After about 10 minutes, place a teaspoon of the basil butter on top of each portion, then add another just before serving.

Lovers' salad ●

THIS IS AN INVITATION TO MAKE A SALAD OF LEAVES CHOSEN FOR THEIR PROPERTIES: mint will freshen the breath, rocket excite the palate, sorrel soothe, lovage clear the mind, lemon balm excite the female, rosemary the male. Add a few flowers for colour and to offset any nervous feelings – nasturtium is the best for this. Olives, if you enjoy them, will add texture and complement the meats. If you can find them, courgette flowers also lift the spirits, and the lemon dressing refreshes the mind.

YOU WILL NEED

FOR THE DRESSING: *1 egg yolk* ● *1 tablespoon Dijon mustard* ● *3 tablespoons fresh lemon juice* ● *100 ml/3½ fl oz olive oil* ● *a little grated lemon zest* ● *leaves from a few stems of rosemary, finely chopped* ● *salt and pepper*

FOR THE SALAD: *Mixed salad leaves, herbs and flowers as above* ● *a few lettuce leaves* ● *1 cucumber, peeled and thickly sliced* ● *a few olives (optional)*

● FIRST MAKE THE DRESSING: WHISK THE EGG YOLK, mustard and lemon juice in a small bowl, then add the oil slowly in a very thin stream (rather like a mayonnaise, but not quite so thick). Add the lemon zest, rosemary and a little seasoning. Chill and allow to steep for a few hours. ● JUST BEFORE SERVING, COMBINE THE SALAD INGREDIENTS AND TOSS WITH THE DRESSING. The flowers should be added last for visual effect: they can even be added after the salad has been dressed, so as not to become wet. The whole meal is designed to be light but full of flavour.

Summer fruit champagne jelly ❦ THE EFFECTS OF THE SCENTS AND

TASTES OF THE PREVIOUS COURSES MEANS YOU MIGHT NOT GET ROUND TO THIS DESSERT. But an item of beauty that adds yet another summer colour dimension and is easily divided at an open-air meal will provide a fabulous crescendo for the meal. You can make this as much as two days ahead for a fuss-free time on the day.

YOU WILL NEED

1 bottle of champagne ❦ *450 g/1 lb caster sugar* ❦ *150 g/5 oz cherries, stems removed* ❦ *3 tablespoons of gelatine* ❦ *1 punnet of raspberries* ❦ *1 punnet of blueberries* ❦ *1 punnet of strawberries* ❦ *1 punnet of mulberries or boysenberries if available* ❦ *½ teaspoon oil, to brush the mould* ❦ *a few borage flowers or violets*

❦ IN A LARGE HEAVY SAUCEPAN, MIX THE CHAMPAGNE AND SUGAR AND BRING RAPIDLY TO THE BOIL. Add the cherries and bring back to the boil – but don't cook too quickly or the cherry skins will split open. Simmer gently for about 5 minutes.

❦ POUR THE CHERRIES AND THE SYRUP INTO A BOWL AND ALLOW TO COOL SLIGHTLY. Dissolve the gelatine in about 100 ml/3½ fl oz hot water, stir this into the cherries and syrup and leave to cool right down. ❦ JUST AS THE MIXTURE BEGINS TO SET A SKIN WILL BEGIN TO FORM; add the berries and stir in gently. ❦ OIL AN ICE-CREAM OR JELLY MOULD AND LADLE IN JUST A LITTLE OF THE SYRUP. Toss in the flowers and a tiny bit of the fruit, then chill until the mixture is lightly set. Add the remaining liquid and fruit and return to the refrigerator, covering with cling film. If possible, leave overnight (or longer) and then unmould onto a plate by first dipping the mould in hot water for a moment. Turn out and cover with film. To serve, remove the film and decorate with fresh flowers.

HEARTH & HOME

A HARVEST CELEBRATION

The Menu (serves 4 plus) • Onion, olive and herb flan • Stuffed guinea fowl in cider and cream • Open fruit tartlets • Blackberry and plum jam • Mulberry jam

This time of the year was known as Mabon, and was the first serious harvest celebration, fixed at the Autumn Equinox (21 September). The sun is starting its autumnal decline, but the earth's bounty is bursting as at no other time of year; as individuals, we should revel in the earth's early maturity and its delicious produce. Starting with the sunny days of September and running into October, these pumpkin-coloured days are associated everywhere with harvest. In the southern hemisphere, this occurs for you in late March.

Celebrating the bounteous harvest 🍎 Spiritually, we can

share the mood of the earth and celebrate, honouring the bounty of the season, looking ahead to continuing luck and good fortune. Our magical tasks bring us close to the earth; we gather the fruits of the late autumn. This is the time for making jams and jellies, infusing them with ingredients for magic-making in the wintry days ahead. We can also plan our celebration feast, which will culminate in Hallowe'en in the following chapter, and use the appropriate fare from this seasonal moment of the earth's goodwill for the next two months. 🍎 This is the best time to begin harvesting herbs in the country, drying them for use in winter and decorating the home while imbuing our environment with wonderful, magical, uplifting smells that trigger positivity in our brains, and act as blessings over our domesticity. If you live in the city, harvest the contents of your flowerpots and window boxes – even on a tiny scale – just to share the merriment of the moment. Decorate your living space with autumnal colours and bunches of grapes, or hops, or sheaves of wheat, or vines; or place gourds and pumpkins around candles to honour the spirits of the season for the weeks ahead.

A home spell 🍎 This is a wonderful moment to enact a blessing on your dwelling

to attract all good thought and feeling, and drive away any negativity or feeling of failure that has gone before. Utilise the wonderful herbs on offer to do this. You might make a small doll out of scraps of rosemary to place in your house and attract good omens; or, if you feel really inspired, strew your house with lavender and mint, and sweep it through from the front door to the back, and return again from back to front, to bring in sparkling sunshine feelings and sweep out the blues. Use an old-fashioned witch's besom, and make wishes and thoughts focus on your intention to drive ahead in the months to come, to focus on tasks until they are complete, and to invite happy thoughts and friends to share your table and your home. Work up a sweat and play some music if it helps. Your house should be zinging when you finish, and you will feel the energy and hope tangibly around you.

Decorative pastry cornucopia centrepiece

YOUR HOME CHANGES MOOD ALONG WITH THE SEASON. Bright summer blooms, where a rose petal beguilingly breaks free from a hand-picked summer bouquet, will now be replaced by dried flowers and herb baskets – but the romance and beauty doesn't have to be compromised at all. Every Mabon I make a table centrepiece which lasts almost until Yule; it is an inedible pastry cornucopia (or horn of plenty), which can then be strewn with last summer/early autumn fruits, or late flower petals. It could as readily be made to use as a place setting, bursting with flowers and a name card, for guests at your Mabon table. THE CORNUCOPIA CELEBRATES THE SPIRIT OF THE SEASON BETTER THAN ANY OTHER SHAPE, but you could adapt your modelling to create a huge conch shell if you live near the sea, or any other shape that takes your creative fancy.

YOU WILL NEED

1 butternut squash ● *225 g/8 oz plain flour* ● *100 g/3½ oz cooking salt* ● *whites of 2 eggs and 1 yolk* ● *a little iced water*

PREHEAT THE OVEN TO ABOUT 150°C/300°F/GAS 2. I use a butternut squash because its shape so nearly resembles the horn of plenty, then I wrap several layers of strong foil around the pumpkin to create a hollow 'mould' of the right shape. Slip the foil carefully off the pumpkin, then use this mould to wrap your pastry around and build up the horn. Then repeat the process with more foil to create a second mould. MIX ALL THE OTHER INGREDIENTS EXCEPT THE EGG YOLK IN A FOOD PROCESSOR WITH JUST ENOUGH WATER TO MAKE A DOUGH, then knead gently on a lightly floured surface. The texture will remain quite tough. Divide this into 2 portions and roll one out to a thickness of about 1 cm/½ inch. Cut the pastry into narrow strips, about 2-3 cm/¾-1¼ inch thick. STARTING AT THE BASE OF THE FOIL CORNUCOPIA, wrap one strip over the bottom, then layer each successive strip over the last. Brush the layers with a little iced water to make them stick. Once the shape is completed, brush the whole with the egg yolk. Repeat this process with the second portion of dough and second mould, so you have two cornucopias. Place them on a baking tray and cook in the slow oven for up to two hours to dry the pastry right out. They are ready when the pastry is a rich golden colour. Set aside to cool completely, and then you can remove the foil. FILL THEM WITH FLOWERS, SWEETS, OR FRUITS, EITHER DUSTED WITH ICING SUGAR OR CRYSTALLISED. The cornucopias look majestic – but don't forget you cannot eat them!

Making pastry from the heart 🍎 MAKING PASTRY IS ONE OF THOSE

CULINARY UNDERTAKINGS INTO WHICH YOU CAN WORK A GREAT DEAL OF MAGICAL EMOTION. It has always been a labour of love – more so now, as commercial pastries and flans, and pre-packaged frozen varieties, are so easy to come by and use. However, think of pastry-making as weaving a magic spell: you have a chance to create some powerful magnetism for your guests and for someone special – so don't pass up that opportunity if you can find the time. My favourite aunt Zena taught me to bake when I was still a child and, as so few people do it now, it is my chance to send love and magic to my family and friends. It is as natural to me as spell-making.

Pâte brisée 🍎 THIS IS THE FRENCH VERSION OF SHORTCRUST PASTRY, and is the best base for myriad

flans and tarts. Put on some music as you work.

YOU WILL NEED

160 g/5½ oz plain flour 🍎 *80 g/3 oz cold butter* 🍎 *a pinch of salt* 🍎 *about 5 tablespoons iced water*

MAKES 1 MEDIUM-SIZED FLAN CASE

🍎 SIFT THE FLOUR INTO A MEDIUM-SIZED BOWL, AND CUT IN THE BUTTER WITH A SHARP KNIFE. Rub the small pieces of the butter through the flour with your fingertips, using the gentlest caress you would apply to your lover. The mixture should resemble fine breadcrumbs. Add a pinch of salt and then, little by little, just enough iced water to make a paste. When the dough makes a ball but doesn't stick to your fingers, it is ready. Chill for an hour and then roll out on a floured surface. Work your love in thoughts not deeds, for you must not over-handle the pastry: it is a good metaphor for love.

Sweet pastry cooked in a pan

My husband loves this easy variation of Pate Brisée because it never gets soggy. The technique of mixing the ingredients in a pan over heat ensures a delicious crisp result – and you don't have to worry about baking it blind. Use it for sweet pies and flans, such as wild strawberry, or pumpkin pie, the perfect dish for this season.

You will need

150 g/5 oz butter ● 75 g/2¾ oz caster sugar ● 225 g/8 oz plain flour

Melt the butter over low heat in a saucepan, then add the sugar and stir until it is incorporated. Sift in the flour and stir with a wooden spoon until a nice ball forms in the pan. Allow to cool, then chill a little, so that it is ready to press into a 20 cm/8 inch flan dish. As it dries out in the dish, it becomes very crisp and firm. Think lovingly over it, as you employ your fingers in the task of pressing it into the dish.

Wholemeal pastry cooked in a pan

This third variation also uses the method described above, so the pastry is wonderfully flaky and never soggy, and is ideal for a savoury flan. This will make enough pastry for a flan that will serve as a starter for eight, or a main course for four. You can use half white and half wholemeal flour if you prefer a lighter texture.

You will need

200 g/7 oz butter, plus more for greasing the tin ● 100 ml/3½ fl oz milk ● 225 g/8 oz self-raising wholemeal flour

Gently heat the butter with the milk and stir in until they are combined and the butter completely melted. Add your flour and mix as above, until a large ball forms in the saucepan. While it is still warm (but not too hot to touch), press this pastry into the base of a greased 25 cm/10 inch flan tin.

Onion, olive and herb flan

THE COMBINATION OF FLAVOURS HERE IS REDOLENT OF THE LONG, HOT MEDITERRANEAN SUMMER. The easy wholemeal pastry described above makes the perfect base for this flan.

YOU WILL NEED

3 teaspoons chopped mixed fresh herbs (marjoram, thyme and tarragon are most suitable) ● *600 ml/1 pint double cream* ● *5 garlic cloves (in their skins)* ● *2 onions, thinly sliced* ● *1 tablespoon olive oil* ● *4 eggs, lightly beaten* ● *a few pitted black or green olives*

● PREHEAT THE OVEN TO 180°C/350°F/GAS 4. Simmer the herbs very gently in the cream for several minutes. Remove from the heat and set aside to allow the flavours to develop. ● ROAST THE UNPEELED GARLIC CLOVES IN THE WARM OVEN FOR ABOUT 20 MINUTES, UNTIL SOFT AND FRAGRANT. Remove them from the oven but leave the oven on. When the cloves are cool enough to handle, peel off the skins and mash the garlic into the cream and herb mixture. ● SAUTÉ THE ONIONS IN THE OLIVE OIL UNTIL TRANSLUCENT, THEN SPREAD OVER THE BASE OF THE PASTRY. Mix the eggs well with the cream mixture, then pour over the onions. Finally, dot the olives over the surface. Bake in the oven for up to 40 minutes until the filling is firm on top. ● SERVE WHILE STILL WARM.

Stuffed guinea fowl in cider and cream • This is

A VERY OLD ENGLISH WEST COUNTRY RECIPE AND REMINDS US OF THE MAGICAL PROPERTIES OF CIDER, with its "last oozings, hours by hours", as described by Keats. This dish is ideal for a harvest celebration, as it is a little special and takes advantage of perfect seasonal produce. If you can't get a guinea fowl, substitute a game bird such as a pheasant or a free-range or corn-fed chicken.

YOU WILL NEED

225 g/8 oz sausage meat • 4 onions, sliced • ½ teaspoon cinnamon • a few mushrooms, chopped • 2 small apples, peeled, cored and roughly chopped • 1 guinea fowl or game bird or free-range chicken • 4 bacon rashers (optional) • 2 tablespoons olive oil • 200 ml/7 fl oz dry cider • 100 ml/3½ fl oz chicken stock • 2 tablespoons double cream • salt and pepper

• PREHEAT THE OVEN TO 180°C/350°F/GAS 4. Combine the sausage meat, onions, cinnamon, mushrooms and apples in a mixing bowl, then stuff this mixture into the cavity of the bird and secure with skewers or needle and thread. • PUT THE BIRD ON A RACK IN A ROASTING PAN, cover the breast with the bacon if using (otherwise reserve a little sliced onion to put over the breast), then sprinkle over the oil. Pour the cider and stock under and around the bird, then make a loose tent over it with foil to allow the bird to steam. • COOK IN THE OVEN FOR ABOUT 30 MINUTES, then remove the foil and cook for 30 minutes more to brown the bird. Baste it with the pan juices from time to time. • REMOVE THE GUINEA FOWL FROM THE OVEN AND SET ASIDE IN A WARM PLACE TO REST FOR AT LEAST 10 MINUTES BEFORE CARVING. Reduce the pan juices by one-third over high heat, then stir in the cream and salt and pepper to taste. • SERVE THE GUINEA FOWL WITH THE CREAM SAUCE HANDED ROUND SEPARATELY. Mashed potatoes and root vegetables flavoured with herbs make the perfect accompanying vegetables.

Open fruit tartlets

THIS IS AN OPPORTUNITY TO WEAVE BLESSINGS AND LUCK INTO YOUR DESSERT AGAIN, to wish bounty and harmony on all. Late-season strawberries are a last fling from the warm weather, but any other soft fruit is lovely, and apples are especially good at this time – so try any filling you like.

YOU WILL NEED

FOR THE PASTRY SHELLS: *115 g/4 oz butter, plus more for greasing the tins* ● *115 g/4 oz caster sugar* ● *1 egg* ● *a few drops of vanilla extract* ● *225 g/8 oz plain flour* ● *a pinch of salt*

FOR THE CRÈME ANGLAISE: *2 egg yolks* ● *30 g/1 oz sugar* ● *15 g/½ oz plain flour* ● *125 ml/4 fl oz milk* ● *vanilla extract*

TO SERVE: *12 large strawberries, hulled, or an equivalent quantity of blueberries, clementine segments, or mulberries* ● *a little warmed strawberry or apricot jam*

MAKES 12

● FIRST MAKE THE PASTRY SHELLS: beat the butter and sugar together until creamy, then add the egg and drops of vanilla and combine lightly. Mix in the flour and salt until you have a doughy ball, but do not over-process. Wrap in cling film and chill for about an hour. ● ROLL OUT THE CHILLED DOUGH TO ABOUT 2 MM/^{1}/$_{16}$ INCH IN THICKNESS and cut out 12 rounds with a 6 cm/2½ inch cutter. Lightly grease 12 small tartlet tins and line them with the pastry. Allow to rest in the refrigerator for about 20 minutes. Preheat the oven to 180°C/350°F/Gas 4. ● PRICK THE BASES OF THE TARTLET SHELLS LIGHTLY WITH A FORK AND BAKE FOR ABOUT 10 MINUTES, UNTIL NICELY GOLDEN. Allow to cool.

● TO MAKE THE CRÈME ANGLAISE: mix together the egg yolks and sugar until thick and pale yellow. Add the flour and beat lightly. Bring the milk to the boil in a pan and add about half of it to the egg mixture. Beat well, then add this back to the remaining milk in the pan. Bring the whole mixture to a gentle boil, and whisk throughout. Cook gently for a further two minutes, add a few drops of vanilla and allow to cool completely. ● CAREFULLY SPOON THE CREAMY CUSTARD INTO THE TARTLET CASES, arrange the strawberry halves or other fruit overlapping on top. Brush the top of each fruit-filled tartlet with a little warmed jam, let the glaze cool and set, then serve.

Blackberry and plum jam •

THIS IS A LINK WITH THE WOMEN OF OUR PAST, as the most important preparation for the cold weather ahead lay in the preserving of the late-summer and autumn fruits. Jams and jellies make the most wonderful autumnal edible gifts to spread your magic away from home. Seal with a little spell for happiness, love or luck. Choose any flavours you love or fruits to which you have access.

YOU WILL NEED

1 kg/2¹/₄ lb blackberries • 1 kg/2¹/₄ lb plums • 1.4 kg/3 lb preserving sugar

• CAREFULLY PICK OVER THE FRUIT FOR STEMS AND IMPERFECT BITS. Halve the plums and take out the stones. • PLACE ALL THE FRUIT IN A PRESERVING PAN WITH 300 ML/¹/₂ PINT WATER, BRING GENTLY TO THE BOIL, AND SIMMER FOR ABOUT 10 MINUTES. Now add the sugar and stir until completely dissolved. Sing while you work – and encircle your family and loved ones with light and health. Meanwhile, bring the contents of the pan to the boil and simmer rapidly until you reach setting point (the mixture will coat the back of a spoon). • POT THE WARM JAM IN CLEAN, STERILISED JARS, add wax seals and cover. Allow to cool, then store.

• VARIATIONS: keep the fruit-to-sugar ratio the same, and substitute strawberries or raspberries for the blackberries, and apples or pears for plums. (700 g/1 lb 9 oz very tart green apples will balance 1 kg/2¹/₄ lb soft fruit.)

Mulberry jam •

MULBERRIES ARE MY FAVOURITE SOFT FRUIT, and I love my mulberry tree as no other in my garden. Symbol of wisdom and patience (the tree puts out no leaves till all danger of frost is past), the wonderful red of the fruit stains your mouth and fingers as you raid the tree in autumn for its bounty. Make mulberry jam to partake of wisdom, to cure wintry ailments, and to provide friends with a taste sensation they will get nowhere else. The jam is divine on scones on autumn afternoons. • MAKE EXACTLY AS FOR THE BLACKBERRY AND PLUM JAM ABOVE, but with 2 kg/4¹/₂ lb mulberries, 1.5 kg/3¹/₄ lb preserving sugar and adding only 150 ml/¹/₄ pint water.

THE MENU (SERVES 8 OR MULTIPLY AS YOU NEED) ♣ Homemade
'Damper' Bread ♣ Spicy Autumn Pumpkin Soup ♣ Lamb cooked
in a Brick with Lavender and Hay ♣ Spicy Apple Cake with Vanilla
Cream Sauce ♣ Ginger Divination Biscuits

GOOD LUCK

A HALLOWE'EN SUPPER

Hallowe'en actually celebrates the old Celtic New Year, and the onset of true winter. So here we celebrate the preparations for an old-style 'New Year', including the games and divinations that were traditional to see what the new year would bring. The Celts called this Samhain (pronounced *sow-wane*) – and our Hallowe'en supper could be the conclusion of a night out on the town, or a simple acknowledgment of the onset of winter and the marking of the earth's seasons. In either case, invite friends, have fun, and see what you can expect in the coming year....

Festivals of fire and light ● DECORATIONS FOR HALLOWE'EN ARE WIDELY

KNOWN: the pumpkin (or originally turnip) lanterns, the ghoulish masks, the parodies of witches and demons who were supposed to stand guardian over the kingdom of spirits, the bonfires, and the fancy dress. Perhaps here we can go back to what is less known – the truly celebratory aspect of a new year, with fireworks and beacons and laughter and parties. In Britain the creation of Guy Fawkes stole considerably from the previously Celtic and Catholic feasts of Samhain and Hallowe'en. For making magic, we should restore the celebration of fire and lights – the fireworks and bright colours – which are preserved in many festivals around the country: the November carnivals in Somerset, where I live, are just one of these leftovers. The floodlit floats enacting tableaux are a reminder of the festivals of fire-lighting that were an invitation to stay warm and call back the dying sun, to endure the cold weather. In these ancient ceremonies, the ghouls had a smaller share of the partying. ● THE SPIRIT REVELLERS WHO WANTED TO COMMUNE WITH THE ANCESTRAL SPIRITS LEARNED HERBAL AND GEM LORE FROM THEM, RETURNING THE KNOWLEDGE TO THE COMMUNITY. These were the witches, who had second sight, for whom this feast period was a doorway between worlds and wisdoms. So, if you choose to dress as a witch, you have a great responsibility to share your knowledge, wisdom and healing with others. ● THE FEAST TABLES WERE LAID FOR THE ANCESTORS AND THE SPIRITS OF THE EARTH, who brought forth the bounty. This is an honouring of the divine. Lay your table with care. ● MAKE GREAT POTTERY OR EARTHENWARE VASES, AND FILL THEM WITH THE FRUITING STEMS OF PLUMS OR GOOSEBERRIES FOR YOUR HOME. Remember that apples were sacred to the goddess (when cut in half crosswise, they have her 'star' in the centre). Also, the colour red celebrated the life force and energy – so apples may well be the perfect choice for a table centrepiece. If you're lucky enough to have access to rowan berries, they, too, are a perfect colour celebration of the season. ● SPRAY APPLES GOLDEN – AND LEAVE A LEAF ATTACHED. This ensures gold in your purse, and life stemming from it. Place them in a glass dish or bowl, to make the connection with the fire through which the glass has passed. As you decorate, sing songs of continued bounty – or simply see little visions of success (though not only monetary). ● MAKE A LITTLE 'INVITATION' TO BENEVOLENCE FOR CALLERS AT YOUR DOOR: create a beautiful wreath (the emblem of open house) with bunches of blueberries or currants tied in amongst the foliage. The frosty days will preserve them wonderfully – and some people like to think of this as 'fairy food', to bestow little blessings on the dwellers in the house. A basket laden with apples, melon, plums and quinces, placed at porch, door or hall, will invite an uplifting smile from your guests and also a gesture of luck from the earth and divine spirits who appreciate your gesture of thanks. If your love life needs a little extra good blessing, make sure to include a quince – the love apple – specially favoured by the goddess Aphrodite.

Autumn colour ✹ PUMPKINS ARE A VITAL SYMBOL OF THE AUTUMN HARVEST AND

HALLOWE'EN. These wonderful, warm-coloured squashes have a heart, it seems, and make delightful shapes when hollowed out and carved, filled with candles (use safe night-lights), placed in windows, on porches, steps or in gardens. They also look fabulous tottering off a garden wall or balcony, stacked in piles of different varieties and sizes. ✹ FOR DECORATION AT YOUR WINTER/NEW YEAR FEAST, SCOOP MOST OF THE FLESH OUT OF A LARGE PUMPKIN AND FILL WITH CHRYSANTHEMUMS. The sight will completely lift your soul, and honour every essence in nature – either conventionally religious, pagan, or just Wordsworthian. Or find little nugget pumpkins and tie a name card to each of their stems as place settings for your Hallowe'en feast table. If you want to do this year after year, varnishing the pumpkins would be time well spent.

Varnishing gourds ✹ MAKE MAGIC WHILE YOU VARNISH A GOURD: this is the symbol of

a happy earth in balance with the seasons and human endeavour. You need to pick a gourd (pumpkins of so many sorts, including little nuggets, butternuts or large calabash gourds, in colours ranging from green or yellow to fiery reds and oranges) when they are fully ripe. Check that the stem itself feels dry, and leave at least 5 cm/2 inches of stem when you cut the fruit. Wipe it well, then make a tiny pinprick hole in the base and at the top of the gourd. Now you must store it somewhere cool and dry, with a rack underneath – or if you have enough stem, hang it up by this. It takes at least a month to dry out your gourd – and considerably longer if you have a large pumpkin. You know it is dried out properly when it feels light to lift and you can probably hear the seeds moving around inside. ✹ ONCE IT HAS DRIED, COAT THE GOURD WITH CLEAR VARNISH, WHICH WILL KEEP THE BEAUTIFUL COLOURS BRIGHT. If you varnish an unripe gourd you will soon find it rots and leaves a bitter smell – so it's best not to rush the process. Pile your varnished gourds up together in baskets or trays, on chairs and shelves, or put them on pretty plates on a table or altar, or even by the fireside (but not too close). If you have storage space, they will keep for a long time.

Homemade 'damper' bread ❀ BREADS ARE THE PERFECT MEDIUM

FOR WORKING MAGIC, AS YOU CAN FOCUS THOUGHTS OF PROSPERITY AND HARMONY AS YOU KNEAD AWAY. They also traditionally crown the celebrations at harvest and form the centre of many harvest feasts. Damper bread, cooked in a flowerpot, is my own special favourite, combining the elements of earth and fire with the food to honour the earth's good spirits. It must also be the easiest bread in the world to make.

YOU WILL NEED

60 g/2 oz butter, plus more for greasing the pots ❀ *350 g/12 oz self-raising flour, plus more for the pots* ❀ *1½ teaspoons salt* ❀
2 tablespoons chopped mixed fresh herbs, including parsley and rosemary ❀ *100 ml/3½ fl oz milk* ❀ *100 ml/3½ fl oz water*

❀ PREHEAT THE OVEN TO 200°C/400°F/GAS 6 and lightly grease the insides of 4 small new and spotlessly clean terracotta flowerpots with butter, then dust them with flour. ❀ SIFT TOGETHER THE FLOUR AND SALT INTO A BOWL. Rub in the butter until the mixture resembles breadcrumbs and then add the herbs. Punch a well in the centre of the mixture and add the milk and the water. Stir lightly, using a knife. When the mixture leaves the edges of the bowl, turn out onto a lightly floured board or table. Knead it a little and, as you do, make your wishes and thoughts focus on prosperity, luck and thanks to the world around you. Now divide the dough into 4 pieces and shape each into a ball. Put each loosely into one of the prepared flowerpots. ❀ BAKE IN THE HOT OVEN FOR 15 MINUTES, or until the bread just rises over the edge of the pot. Serve the bread while still warm, buttered, with pumpkin soup or stew. As you break the bread with your friends, make a short wish – or toast – to prosperity for all.

Pumpkin damper ❀ THIS WONDERFUL VARIATION IS SPECIFIC TO HALLOWE'EN.

❀ ADD 675 G/1½ LB COOKED AND MASHED PUMPKIN TO THE RECIPE AFTER THE BUTTER AND LEAVE OUT THE HERBS. Reduce the milk/water mixture by half or as much as it takes to make a sticky dough; then knead and bake as above.

Spicy autumn pumpkin soup ❦ As the emblem of the season,

this is the quintessential ingredient for a Hallowe'en supper after trick-or-treating the neighbourhood, or a chilly night around the bonfire. It will taste sensational with the spices. You already know from previous chapters that ginger has restorative properties; both this and the garam masala are thought to please the gods. For maximum effect, serve the soup in a 'tureen' cut from a huge pumpkin, scraping out the flesh and seeds.

You will need

750 g/1¾ lb pumpkin ❦ 30 g/1 oz butter ❦ 1 large onion, chopped ❦ 1 cm/½ inch fresh root ginger, peeled and finely chopped ❦ ½ teaspoon garam masala ❦ 3 teaspoons plain flour ❦ 600 ml/1 pint chicken or vegetable stock ❦ salt and pepper ❦ 1 teaspoon chopped chives ❦ 1 teaspoon chopped coriander ❦ 1 tablespoon single cream or yoghurt per person, to serve

❦ Leave the pumpkin unpeeled (much easier) and chop into evenly sized pieces, discarding the seeds. Place the pumpkin in a steamer, cover and steam for 30 minutes. When cool enough to handle, scrape away the flesh from the skin, discard the skin and process the flesh roughly in a blender. ❦ Melt the butter in a large saucepan and sauté the onion in it gently for a few minutes, then add the ginger, garam masala and flour. Cook for a few minutes, stirring continuously. Add the stock, still stirring, and bring to the boil. Reduce the heat and add the pumpkin with some seasoning. Stir until well combined, then cover and simmer gently for about 10 minutes. Add in the fresh herbs and adjust the seasoning to taste.

❦ Pour into a pumpkin tureen as described above. Serve the soup with a tablespoon of cream or yoghurt and with a slice of damper.

Lamb cooked in a brick with lavender and hay

🍎 NOTHING ENCAPSULATES SUMMER IN THE COUNTRY MORE THAN HAYMAKING. As the days shorten and the late sun wanes, this recipe will tease your sense of smell into a little flashback of those long hot summer days. This dish is a magical main course for your Hallowe'en feast, and easy to make for lots of friends. The recipe works best using a terracotta chicken brick, but if you cannot find one, use a heavy lidded casserole.

YOU WILL NEED

1 boned leg or loin of lamb, weighing 2-2½ kg/4-5½ lb 🍎 *2 dozen heads and stalks of lavender* 🍎 *a good handful of fresh clean hay or dried grass* 🍎 *100 g/4 oz butter* 🍎 *salt and pepper to taste* 🍎 *3-4 tablespoons water* 🍎 *1 tablespoon plain flour*

🍎 PREHEAT THE OVEN TO 220°C/425°F/GAS 7. Make half a dozen shallow cuts in the surface of the lamb and insert a lavender head into each. Wash the bunch of hay under cold running water, shake off excess, and allow it to retain some of the water. Bend the hay into a nest shape and place it inside an earthenware chicken brick. Sprinkle the remaining lavender over the hay, reserving some of the prettiest sprigs for garnish. 🍎 SMEAR THE LAMB GENEROUSLY WITH THE BUTTER, AND SEASON WITH PLENTY OF SALT AND PEPPER. Cradle the lamb into the nest of hay, and push it right down into the middle of it. Spoon the water over the lamb, then fit the lid in place. 🍎 BAKE FOR 20 MINUTES PER 450 G/1 LB FOR NICE PINK LAMB, 25 if you prefer it well-done, removing the lid for the last 10 minutes to brown. Transfer the lamb to a warm plate. Using oven mitts, carefully remove the hay from the brick, shaking off any juices back into the base. Strain these juices from the brick into a saucepan, add up to a tablespoon of flour to thicken, and bring to the boil, stirring well. Adjust the seasoning. 🍎 SERVE THE LAMB GARNISHED WITH FRESH LAVENDER SPRIGS AND THE SLIGHTLY THICKENED JUICES IN A WARM SAUCE BOAT.

Spicy apple cake with vanilla cream sauce

THE APPLE IS THE TRADITIONAL EMBLEM OF THE GODDESS, so make a wish as you cut this delicious warm pudding cake.

YOU WILL NEED

FOR THE CAKE: *75 g/2¾ oz soft butter, plus more for greasing the tin* ● *175 g/6 oz granulated sugar, plus more for dusting* ● *1 large egg* ● *175 ml/6 fl oz single cream* ● *200 g/7 oz plain flour* ● *2 teaspoons baking powder* ● *a pinch of salt* ● *½ teaspoon freshly grated nutmeg* ● *½ teaspoon ground cinnamon* ● *½ teaspoon ground ginger* ● *½ teaspoon vanilla extract* ● *grated zest of 1 lemon* ● *3 slightly tart apples* ● *75 g/2¾ oz pecan halves*

FOR THE SAUCE: *500 ml/18 fl oz double cream* ● *115 g/4 oz caster sugar* ● *30 g/1 oz unsalted butter* ● *a little grated lemon zest* ● *½ teaspoon freshly grated nutmeg* ● *½ teaspoon ground cinnamon* ● *1 vanilla pod*

● PREHEAT THE OVEN TO 190°C/375°F/GAS 5. Butter a 20 cm/8 inch springform cake tin or flan dish with a removable base. ● BEAT THE REMAINING BUTTER AND SUGAR TOGETHER UNTIL WELL CREAMED, then add the egg and beat for a few minutes more. Add the cream and beat until the whole mixture is smooth. Combine the flour, baking powder, salt and spices, then add this to the mixture and beat in well. Add the vanilla and lemon zest, and beat until smooth. Pour or spoon the cake batter into the prepared tin or dish and smooth the surface with a knife or spatula. ● PEEL AND CORE THE APPLES AND CUT INTO THINNISH SLICES. Arrange these over the batter in pretty circular patterns, placing pecan halves at intervals in between or in the centre. Dust with a little more sugar. Bake in the preheated oven for about 30 minutes, until the apples are nicely golden on top. Meanwhile, make the sauce. ● COMBINE ALL THE INGREDIENTS IN A HEAVY SAUCEPAN AND BRING GENTLY TO THE BOIL, giving the vanilla pod plenty of time to infuse into the cream. Reduce the heat and cook for a while, whisking from time to time. As the sauce thickens a little, discard the vanilla pod. Cook for about 5 minutes more, but do not allow to boil again. ● CHECK THE CAKE WITH A SKEWER, which should come out clean when the cake is completely baked through. ● ALLOW IT TO COOL IN THE TIN A LITTLE, then slip a knife around the sides and release the springform. Serve while still warm, cut into slices, with the cream sauce spooned over.

Ginger divination biscuits ● AT THE END OF YOUR HALLOWE'EN SUPPER

GIVE YOUR GUESTS SOMETHING TO TAKE HOME FOR LUCK, which can 'prophesy' their future year. Uplifting ginger was the traditional ingredient of 'luck biscuits', offered at medieval fairs. Decorate with some symbolic shapes: small figures – male and female, or even child-sized – can be cut simply with a sharp-pointed knife. Stars would be best made with a cookie cutter, as would the shapes indicating playing card suits. Hearts and diamonds are particularly appropriate for signifying love and business success.

YOU WILL NEED

125 g/4½ oz butter ● *85 g/3 oz brown sugar* ● *1 egg yolk* ● *275 g/10 oz plain flour* ● *1 teaspoon bicarbonate of soda*

● *3 teaspoons ground ginger* ● *2 tablespoons golden syrup* ● *edible gold leaf, to decorate (optional)*

FOR THE ICING: *white of 1 egg* ● *225 g/8 oz icing sugar, sifted* ● *a few drops of lemon juice* ● *a few drops food colouring*

● PREHEAT THE OVEN TO 190°C/375°F/GAS 5. Cream the butter and sugar until light and fluffy, then mix in the egg yolk. Sift in the dry ingredients, followed by the syrup, and mix well, then knead very lightly. ● DIVIDE THIS DOUGH INTO ABOUT FIVE PORTIONS, then roll each portion out between sheets of waxed paper to a thickness of about 3 mm/⅛ inch. Remove the upper layer of waxed paper and cut out some ginger biscuit shapes (see some suggestions above). The ginger biscuit dough does not spread at all, so it will hold in whatever shapes you form. ● LIFT THE FIGURES ONTO BAKING SHEETS WITH THE BOTTOM SHEET OF WAXED PAPER OR CAREFULLY WITH A SPATULA, trying to keep similar sizes together, as larger ones will take a little longer to bake. Bake in the preheated oven for about 7-8 minutes for small shapes and 10 minutes for larger ones. Allow to cool on the trays. ● THE BISCUITS CAN BE ICED AS YOU WISH: beat the egg white lightly, adding the sugar a tablespoon at a time and beating between additions. When the mixture has a good piping consistency, beat in the lemon juice and any colouring. If you prefer, you can spread the icing straight onto the biscuits. ● ALTERNATIVELY, YOU MAY WISH TO DECORATE THEM MORE TRADITIONALLY WITH GOLD LEAF, which adds something really special (available from art and specialist shops: follow the manufacturer's instructions). As you ice or decorate, weave little spells of luck and happiness over the biscuits, so that your friends and family will take on the good magic as they eat them. ● SERVE THE BISCUITS WITH COFFEE, or put them into little cellophane bags, grouped in themes, allowing your guests to pick up a bag blindly and see what the future augurs.

FRIENDS & FAMILY
A YULE FEAST

The Menu (serves 8-10) ❧ Mulled wine ❧ Smoked

salmon parcels with lemon grass sauce ❧ Roast

goose with apples and rum ❧ Potato gratin ❧

Carrots with almonds and honey ❧

Leeks with cream ❧ Florentine

chocolate almond ring

Yule, the pagan ancestor of Christmas, was the mid-winter feast to mark the Winter Solstice on December 21, the day with the shortest hours of daylight after which the light would begin to grow again. To break the austerity of the onset of winter, this time of year became the season of feasts. America preserves the feel of this end-of-autumn/early winter spirit of blessings and familial togetherness with Thanksgiving. The sun was to be encouraged back again – and with it came the kind of New Year that we have inherited. The twin feasts (and you might count all three if you celebrate Thanksgiving too) were a relief from the darkest days. This is a perfect moment for cooking for friends, and wishing them blessings.

Celebrating the circle of life and friendship ◖

This is the perfect moment for cooking for friends, and wishing them blessings. Our chapter takes in a traditional Christmas feast, which could equally be served at Thanksgiving or Yule, or even on New Year's Day. Try to share it with as many dear friends as possible. If family demands prevent you from seeing others you love, reconstruct the pagan feast of Yule (December 21 or 22) as we do, and invite all those who will not be at your Christmas table. This creates a powerful link with our ancestral past, and you will find this special link with the shortest day (or longest if you're an antipodean) very moving. Time seems to stand still at such a moment. ◖ Bring together your friends and family and make magic with your hospitality to banish any sadness and lift their spirits. There is an ebbing of energy at this time of the year for those who dwell in the northern hemisphere – it is like the ebb at three o' clock in the morning, when our tide of human energy is lowest. This meeting of friends and the chance to imbue our paths with positive thoughts and blessings will help us get through the following cold, hard months. Fill the wassail bowl, and light the Yule log; bring in the mistletoe and deck the halls with holly. These symbols of the life force buffer our spirits. ◖ All the recipes here are chosen to give courage to the heart: the smoked salmon (in fact any oily fish) provides zinc and essential oils for vitality; the roast goose may be rich, but the smell and the enjoyment of eating it are uplifting; the vegetable accompaniments and their herbal ingredients are chosen for flavour and fortification against wintry depression (garlic, for instance, wards off infection); and the chocolate and nuts are emblematic both of fertility and sensuousness to restart the life force (be warned). Weave love and magic around all you touch: at this time, the earth and the heavens have a special relationship.

A fireside gathering

For those who are lucky enough to have an open fire, this is when it comes into its own, and it should be central to your decoration. The Yule log was a symbol of the fertility of the flame (sacred to the gods), which was kept alive to ensure the return of the sun after the dark days. Burning resinous woods – such as sandalwood, frankincense, or even juniper and bay – encourages feelings of wellbeing and comfort in those sharing the fireside. Lavish some real care around the hearth if you have one – if not, go mad with candles. Incense made from any of these woods creates a sensuous atmosphere. You can also use multi-wick or pillar candles of fabulous colours. Scent them yourself: allow the candle to burn down for a few minutes, extinguish the flame, then add several drops of your favourite essential oil while the wax is still molten. As it dries back the scent imbues the wax, and will release wonderful aromas when you burn it again. Jasmine and rose oils will recall the heady days of summer; woody cinnamon and benzoin will warm you up in an olfactory way. Place coloured tea lights in little jars on stairs, the hearth, or low tables. For a meditative effect, infuse candles with frankincense, lavender, sandalwood or juniper. For bonhomie, citrus smells, such as bergamot or neroli, will encourage humour and high spirits in your guests. The original Christmas crackers were corn cob husks containing little gifts. Why not revive this tradition: your guests can take them home at the end of the evening – carrying the feelings of goodwill away and out into the world.

Seasonal colour

The colour scheme of red, white and gold denotes luxury, but these traditional Yule and Christmas colours are also deemed to bestow vitality. Red symbolised both the flame and the energy of life, and scientifically we now know that red does, in fact, raise the pulse a little. For Yule (and right through the coldest winter) I spread splashes of red about the house, even altering my usual towels for a few wintry red ones. Buy the odd red chair, or a little red cloth for the tables. Opt for burgundy if red is a little too striking for you. Put red glasses on the table, filled with sweets or flowers. Go wild. Add red cushions or throws to warm the winter beds, and fragrance your rooms with warm woody scents.

Wreaths and swags

These were also a traditional way of injecting living green life and colour into the gloomy year. You could use both fresh and dried herbs amidst other greenery, and decorate doorways, mantles, tables and stairways. I use a base of willow, which is sacred to witches, and is wonderfully flexible for wreaths; other good bases can be woven from hazel. If you have none of these, use a commercial wire or raffia wreath base. USE BAY, MYRTLE, PINE OR OTHER EVERGREEN, SUCH AS EUCALYPTUS, and tie into the wreath base with good florists' wire. Keep the branches of a uniform length and face them all in one direction until the frame is covered. Then tie in other sections of herbs or winter flowers (choose those that will still look nice as they dry out), and add in some cinnamon sticks or Christmas decorations at intervals. Add the dried herbs first, then the fresh. Use the wire as you go, and tie in some ribbon for extra colour and effect. A KITCHEN SWAG MIGHT BOAST CHILLIES, TINY KUMQUATS OR OTHER CHRISTMAS FRUITS, CHERRIES, GOLD-PAINTED APPLES, AND EVEN FAT BULBS OF GARLIC. In the living area, choose pine cones, cinnamon sticks, pretty flowers and tiny Christmas packages. THINK AND SPEAK OF LOVE WHILE YOUR FINGERS ARRANGE THE GREENERY: SAY NOTHING DETRIMENTAL OF ANYONE YOU KNOW, and expect only good things to blossom in the coming year. Speak of no heartbreak or misery – place past disappointments squarely behind you, and weave a dream of love and joy as you swag along.

Mulled wine THIS IS A BRILLIANT EXCUSE TO INVITE FRIENDS TO HELP YOU WITH YOUR SEASONAL DECORATIONS. While you work, the warm spicy wine will help you to weave in a little intoxicating magic.

YOU WILL NEED

2 cinnamon sticks • *1 tablespoon juniper berries* • *grated zest and juice of 1 orange* • *a pinch of freshly grated nutmeg* • *a few cloves* • *1 bottle of red wine* • *demerara or raw cane sugar*

STEEP ALL THE INGREDIENTS TOGETHER FOR ABOUT AN HOUR, then bring the whole mixture very gently to the boil. Take it off the heat after the first bubble, or you will lose the potency of the alcohol. Add sugar to your own taste. SERVE IN FLOWING CUPS AND WITH SHAKESPEAREAN SPIRIT.

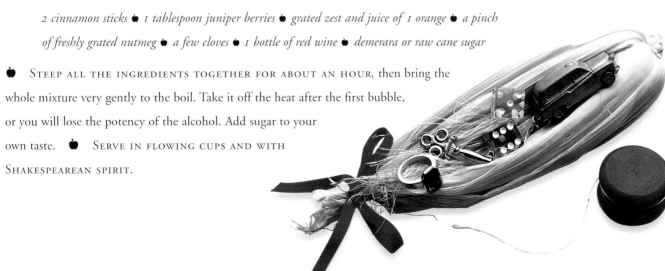

Smoked salmon parcels with lemon grass sauce

🍎 ADD A TOUCH OF THAI FLAVOUR TO THE TRADITIONAL RUSSIAN MIX OF BLINIS AND SALMON.

YOU WILL NEED

8-10 large slices of smoked salmon 🍎 *about 200 ml/7 fl oz crème fraîche* 🍎 *8-10 long chive stalks* 🍎 *1 small jar of salmon roe*

FOR THE LEMON GRASS SAUCE: *30 g/1 oz shallots* 🍎 *1 tablespoon olive oil* 🍎 *2 tablespoons white wine* 🍎 *2 tablespoons vegetable stock* 🍎 *250 ml/9 fl oz double cream* 🍎 *a few stalks of fresh lemon grass*

FOR THE BLINIS: *3 potatoes, peeled and roughly chopped* 🍎 *2 tablespoons plain flour* 🍎 *1 tablespoon chopped chives* 🍎 *2 large eggs* 🍎 *a pinch of mustard powder* 🍎 *1 tablespoon horseradish cream* 🍎 *salt and pepper* 🍎 *3 tablespoons double cream* 🍎 *olive oil, for frying and greasing the moulds*

🍎 FIRST MAKE THE SAUCE: sauté the shallots in a little oil for a few minutes, but do not allow to burn. Add the wine and stock, bring to the boil, and reduce the liquid by about a third (this will take a few minutes). Take off the heat, allow to cool for a minute, then stir in the cream and reheat gently. Add the lemon grass and cook on a very low heat until the mixture has a sauce-like texture. Season to taste. Either put the sauce through a processor to smooth, or aerate with an electric beater.

🍎 TO MAKE THE BLINIS: put the potatoes, flour, chopped chives, eggs, mustard powder, horseradish and some seasoning into a food processor and blend until smooth. Add the cream and lightly incorporate (just a few seconds of processing). Allow to rest for about 20 minutes. 🍎 HEAT A CRÊPE PAN (OR NON-STICK FRYING PAN), add a little oil and stand some lightly oiled round pastry cutters in the pan and pour in sufficient batter to cover the bottom of each mould. Cook the blinis over a high heat for a couple of minutes until the undersides are golden brown, then remove the moulds, turn over and cook the other sides for a minute or until golden. Do this in batches until you have made 8-10 blinis. Keep warm.

🍎 TO ASSEMBLE THE PARCELS: place a slice of salmon on a cutting board, put a blini on top, followed by a spoonful of crème fraîche, then wrap the salmon around the fillings. Secure the salmon parcel with a chive stalk tied in a little knot. 🍎 SPOON SOME LEMON GRASS SAUCE ONTO EACH PLATE, put a smoked salmon parcel on it and on top of the parcel place a teaspoonful of salmon eggs.

Roast goose with apples and rum ❧ IN A FORMER AGE, THE

GOOSE WAS REGARDED NOT JUST AS DELICIOUS MEAT, BUT ALSO SIGNIFIED THE SPIRIT OF SOMETHING WILD THAT RAN BACK TO THE SUN. For this reason, there is a special significance in having roast goose as the main course of your Solstice celebration. The sage helps in the digestion of the fatty meat.

YOU WILL NEED

1 large goose (about 4 kg/9 lb) ❧ *3 tablespoons olive oil* ❧ *about 200 ml/7 fl oz apple brandy (calvados)* ❧ *a little fresh orange and lemon juice* ❧ *a little rum*

FOR THE STUFFING: *6 apples, peeled, cored and sliced* ❧ *200 ml/7 fl oz rum* ❧ *a few sage leaves, finely chopped* ❧ *a pinch of freshly grated nutmeg* ❧ *350 g/12 oz breadcrumbs* ❧ *1 large onion, finely chopped* ❧ *100 g/3½ oz sausage meat* ❧ *salt and pepper*

❧ FIRST MAKE THE STUFFING: soak the apples in the rum for a few hours, then mix this with all the other ingredients and stuff the mixture into the body of the bird. If there is any left over, put it in the crop of the bird. Preheat the oven to 190°C/375°F/Gas 5. ❧ PLACE THE GOOSE ON A RACK IN A BAKING TIN, PRICK THE SKIN IN SEVERAL PLACES AND RUB IT WITH OIL. Sprinkle with salt and pepper, cover with foil and cook in the preheated oven for about 40 minutes per kilo/2¼ lb plus 20 minutes for the stuffing – about 3 hours in total. Baste with the calvados at least every half hour. Remove the foil for the last 20 minutes, to allow the goose to brown. Remove from the oven and allow to rest for at least 15 minutes in a warm place.

❧ MEANWHILE, MAKE THE GRAVY: pour off the excess fat from the roasting tin, then boil the pan juices on the hob, stirring and scraping. Add the citrus juices and a little extra rum and calvados if required for volume. Allow it to bubble, until reduced by about a third, then put in a warmed gravy boat. To honour the sun and set the faces around the table alight, take the goose to the table and spoon over a ladleful of warmed rum. Very carefully set it alight: it will burn briefly. This is the traditional Yule goose.

Potato gratin

❧ THIS MAKES A WONDERFUL CHANGE FROM THE EXPECTED ROAST POTATOES, and the thyme and garlic also help you to digest the large meal.

YOU WILL NEED

2 garlic cloves ❧ *1 kg/2 ¼ lb potatoes, thinly sliced* ❧ *salt and pepper* ❧ *a pinch of freshly grated nutmeg* ❧ *1 large bunch of thyme, with the leaves stripped off the stalks* ❧ *2-3 bay leaves* ❧ *1 teaspoon of butter* ❧ *a little chicken stock*

❧ RUB THE INSIDES OF A MEDIUM-SIZED GRATIN DISH WITH A GARLIC CLOVE. Place slices of potatoes in the dish, overlapping them. When one layer is complete, sprinkle with salt and pepper, a little nutmeg and some of the thyme leaves, then continue to make more layers in the same way. After all the potatoes are used up, crunch the bay leaves on top and scatter the remaining herbs and garlic clove, sliced, and 2-3 dots of butter. Then add just enough stock to cover the bottom of the dish. Cook low down in the oven with the roast goose for the last 45 minutes to 1 hour. Remove from the oven when all the stock has been absorbed and keep warm while you prepare the carrots as below.

Carrots with almonds and honey

❧ THE HONEY AND ALMOND FLAVOURS ARE TRADITIONAL SYMBOLS OF BOUNTY. This should ensure that you have a bountiful year yourself.

YOU WILL NEED

3 large carrots, sliced (not too thinly) ❧ *salt and pepper to taste* ❧ *30 g/1 oz butter* ❧ *3 tablespoons honey* ❧ *125 g/4 ½ oz flaked almonds, toasted for a few minutes in the oven*

❧ PARBOIL THE CARROTS FOR A FEW MOMENTS IN A PAN OF SALTED BOILING WATER. Drain well. ❧ HEAT THE BUTTER IN A FRYING PAN AND SAUTÉ THE CARROT SLICES FOR A FEW MINUTES OVER LOW HEAT. Stir in the honey, followed by the almonds. Allow the almonds to 'candy' for a moment, then remove, season to taste and serve immediately.

Leeks with cream

YOU WILL NEED

1 kg/2 ¼ lb leeks, well rinsed and cut in half lengthwise ● *salt and pepper to taste* ● *45 g/1 ½ oz butter* ● *25 g/¾ oz flour* ● *about 200 ml/7 fl oz milk* ● *a pinch of freshly grated nutmeg* ● *a pinch of paprika* ● *a pinch of cayenne pepper* ● *1 tablespoon chopped fresh oregano* ● *100 ml/3 ½ fl oz double cream* ● *300 g/10 ½ oz Cheddar cheese, grated*

● COOK THE LEEKS IN A LARGE PAN OF SALTED BOILING WATER UNTIL JUST SOFT. Drain well and place in a small casserole or gratin dish. ● MELT HALF THE BUTTER IN A SMALL SAUCEPAN OVER A LOW HEAT, then remove from the heat and add the flour, stirring continually until incorporated. Return to the heat and gradually add the milk. The sauce will thicken. Continue stirring and, at the first bubble, add the remaining butter, little by little and stirring constantly. You may need a drop more milk. When the butter has completely melted and become incorporated, the béchamel sauce is ready. Remove from the heat, stir in the spices and oregano, followed gradually by the cream. Season to taste. ● POUR THE MIXTURE OVER THE LEEKS AND SPRINKLE OVER THE CHEDDAR CHEESE. Bake with the goose, next to the potatoes, for the last 25 minutes.

Florentine chocolate almond ring •

THIS IS A CHRISTMAS CAKE WITH A DIFFERENCE. However, we can still use the magical elements that go into a traditional festive pudding – the charms for luck, the wishes for a prosperous New Year that go into the baking.

YOU WILL NEED

200 g/7 oz unsalted butter, plus more for greasing the tin • *100 g/3½ oz shelled almonds or walnut halves* • *100 g/3½ oz shelled hazelnuts* • *200 g/7 oz dark chocolate (min 50% cocoa solids)* • *6 eggs, separated* • *200 g/7 oz caster sugar* • *few small silver charms or coins*

FOR THE ICING: *200 g/7 oz dark chocolate* • *45 g/1½ oz butter* • *150 ml/¼ pint double cream* • *candied orange slices and cherries, to decorate (optional)* • *crème fraîche or double cream, to serve (optional)* • *a little Grand Marnier, to serve (optional)*

• PREHEAT THE OVEN TO 180°C/350°F/Gas 4. Grease a ring-shaped cake tin, about 26 cm/10½ inches in diameter, with a little of the butter then line it with baking parchment. Place the nuts on a baking tray and toast in the oven for about 15 minutes. Rub the nuts in a tea towel to remove the skins. Reserving some whole nuts for decoration, put the rest in a food processor and chop to a coarse consistency. • CUT THE CHOCOLATE AND THE REMAINING BUTTER INTO SMALL PIECES AND MELT GENTLY IN THE MICROWAVE OR IN A BOWL SET OVER HOT WATER. Stir gently until well mixed. Meanwhile, beat the egg yolks with sugar until creamy. Fold in the nuts, followed by the chocolate mixture and finally a few small silver charms or coins. In a separate bowl, beat the egg whites until quite stiff. Carefully fold the egg whites into the mixture, a little at a time. Then spoon the mixture carefully into the prepared tin, make the surface level and bake in the oven for about 40 minutes, until the top bounces back when prodded but the middle remains a little moist. Allow to cool in the tin for 5 minutes, then turn out onto a rack. • To MAKE THE ICING: melt the chocolate and butter with the cream at a low setting in the microwave or in a bowl over hot water as above until the mixture is completely smooth, then set aside to allow it to cool a little. Pour the icing over the cake, using a spatula to make gentle circular swirls around it. The icing will harden quite quickly. Finish the cake with candied orange slices or cherries interspersed with whole toasted almonds or walnuts and hazelnuts. • To SERVE THE RING, slice with a knife dipped into hot water to cut through the chocolate glaze. It is delicious with a spoonful of crème fraîche or double cream whipped with just a little Grand Marnier. Always make a wish when you cut a ring cake – the shape is like the goddess's crown. Don't forget to warn your guests about the silver pieces inside the cake.

HEALTH
VEGETARIAN VITALITY

8

THE MENU (RECIPES SERVE 2) 🍎 "The milk of paradise" 🍎 Banana

sultana smoothie 🍎 Iced ginger coffee 🍎 Red pepper and spicy tomato

soup 🍎 Vichyssoise of courgettes, leek and potato

(RECIPES SERVE 6) 🍎 Pasta pisanelli 🍎 Cheese and herb fondue

🍎 Lavender panna cottas with rosewater syrup

This moment in the calendar year falls under the Birch Moon, the moon of beginnings; appropriately, it is often the time when we feel the need to cleanse our systems of the richness of the festive season. Many of us pledge diets and detox regimes, try to get fit again, and generally lock horns with winter illnesses if we live in the northern hemisphere. Equally, I well remember those languid, January days in Australia when the heat is turned right up and the humidity can be immense: so I think fresh starts and the need for engaging actively with the weather is apt on both sides of the equator. Here is a selection of healthy veggie recipes that could form the core of a month's healthy eating plan wherever you are. The question is, are there any tricks for staying on the right side of our New Year's resolutions?

Fresh spring energy for body and mind ✿ BEAT THOSE

WINTER BLUES WITH THE ENERGISING AND MEDICINAL VITALITY OF FRESH VEGETABLES AND, AT THE SAME TIME, BRING A FEELING OF SUNSHINE INTO CHILLY DAYS. This is the time when New Year's resolutions have been made, and fresh vegetables are good both for health, detoxing and slimming. ✿ WHATEVER MY PLEDGE, to stay on course I light a sunshine-coloured candle, write my aim on a little square of paper underneath, and burn it for an hour or so each day until my routine is established. This helps, whether you are trying to deal with a piled-high work table, or an exercise regime, or just whittling away a few excess pounds. It would work just as well for a plan to quit smoking, clean out or redecorate the house. ✿ KEEPING WINTER ILLS AT BAY IS LARGELY A CASE OF MIND OVER MATTER: make a little pool of healthy light to dwell in, and keep those gremlin viruses away. If you do succumb to a bug, attack it mentally as well as physically. Imagine some little nuisance critter gnawing away at your healthy cells – and imagine your pool of light and your energising diet swallowing the virus up. Worked in tandem with other cures, this will tip the scales from lingering maladies to short-lived health problems – especially if your system is tired. ✿ IT'S A CRISP, FRESH, FROSTY JANUARY DAY AS I WRITE, SO THIS CHAPTER IS FROM THE HEART. These recipes will work well in southern climes, though – where in the northern winter they would be eaten hot, in the southern summer many can be served cold. ✿ SO, HERE WE HAVE A MAGICAL COLLECTION OF DISHES WHICH COULD FORM THE MENU FOR A HEALTH-FANATIC'S DINNER PARTY, OR JUST THE CORE OF A HEALTHY EATING PLAN. But everyone needs their fun and you'll still want to see your friends, so there are a few recipes that can be shared, plus one temptingly delicious dessert. A fondue is included for one special but unusual focus of entertaining – and though the cheese could be rich, the quantity you actually eat is minimal. Here's to the moon of new beginnings...

Vitamins and minerals from the juice bar 🍎

FRESHLY SQUEEZED FRUIT AND VEGETABLE JUICES BOMBARD YOUR TIRED BODY WITH WONDERFUL VITAMINS, and are one of the best ways of keeping winter ills at bay or dealing with the lingering tiredness of this long season. It is best to invest in a really efficient juicing machine (available in shiny chrome from many outlets) and remember always that the fruits and vegetables you use should be organic if possible – after all, you are what you eat. 🍎 THE BEST COMBINATION OF ALL IS CARROT AND APPLE, sometimes with a little fresh ginger and some freshly squeezed lemon juice added: a veritable vitamin bomb which will give your system a rocket boost of energy and health. 🍎 BUT THINK OF FRESH JUICES ALSO AS A WAY OF IMBIBING THE SUN AND THE EXOTIC, RESTORING YOUR SPIRIT WITH COLOUR AND TASTE. Gather a selection of tropical fruits and make yourself a blissful cocktail of their sweet juices – just shut your eyes as you drink and imagine yourself on a warm tropical beach. 🍎 IF YOU'RE SLIMMING, WATCHING YOUR CHOLESTEROL OR DETOXING, SOME OF THE RECIPES THAT FOLLOW WOULD FORM A MEAL ON THEIR OWN; but if you're entertaining, they make novel starters. The glasses will look wonderful if you put them in the freezer for 20 minutes before serving: they frost majestically when removed.

"The milk of paradise" 🍎 THIS IS THE POET COLERIDGE'S DESCRIPTION OF THE

BLESSED SOUL IN REVERIE, WHO "ON HONEYDEW HATH FED". It is the best start for a New Year clean-out, and can be made virtually fat-free – in fact, with less than 5 g of fat. It should be prepared just before it is to be served.

YOU WILL NEED

250 g/9 oz honeydew melon, peeled, deseeded and chopped 🍎 *1 tablespoon skimmed milk powder* 🍎 *1 tablespoon lime juice* 🍎
2 tablespoons buttermilk or low-fat yoghurt 🍎 *1 teaspoon honey* 🍎 *crushed ice cubes* 🍎 *2 strawberries, to decorate*

SERVES 2

🍎 PROCESS ALL THE INGREDIENTS EXCEPT THE STRAWBERRIES TOGETHER IN A BLENDER UNTIL THEY ARE SMOOTH AND CREAMY. Decorate with a fresh strawberry on the edge of each glass.

Banana sultana smoothie 🍎 THIS WHIP IS RICHER IN CALORIES THAN THE

PREVIOUS DRINK, but you can make it a meal in itself, and it still has a fat content of less than 5 g. It is a good choice if you're very tired.

YOU WILL NEED

250 ml/9 fl oz skimmed milk 🍎 *juice of 1 lemon* 🍎 *1 large banana, sliced* 🍎 *1 tablespoon sultanas* 🍎 *1 tablespoon wheatgerm* 🍎 *2 tablespoons honey* 🍎 *a pinch of ground cinnamon* 🍎 *a pinch of freshly grated nutmeg* 🍎 *crushed ice cubes* 🍎 *sprig of mint, to decorate*

SERVES 2

🍎 RESERVING 2 SLICES OF BANANA, process all ingredients together in a blender until smooth. Pour into glasses, put a drinking straw through each of the reserved banana slices and decorate with a sprig of mint to serve.

Iced ginger coffee 🍎 GINGER HAS POWERFUL MEDICINAL QUALITIES, giving you a zing

of energy and also helping to fight off infection, particularly anything bronchial. Here's a mock cappuccino for those who find it difficult to give up their milky breakfast treat.

YOU WILL NEED

1 small cup of strong coffee 🍎 *2 tablespoons boiling water* 🍎 *250 ml/9 fl oz skimmed milk* 🍎 *3 pinches of ground ginger* 🍎 *1 tablespoon ginger ice-cream* 🍎 *crushed ice cubes*

SERVES 2

🍎 RESERVING 2 PINCHES OF GINGER, process all the ingredients together until smooth, then pour into 2 glasses and dust the tops of each with the reserved ginger.

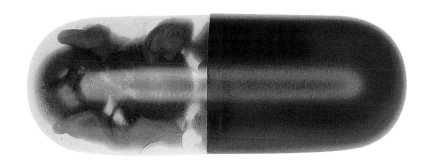

Soothing soups

🍎 THIS IS A WAY OF PUTTING THE SAME VITALITY THAT WAS IN THE GLASS IN THE PREVIOUS RECIPES INTO A BOWL AND WARMING IT UP. Soup is brilliant for slimming, fights off both lethargy and viruses, and is the ultimate soothing comfort food when you're feeling under the weather. 🍎 OVER THE PAGE YOU WILL FIND TWO DELICIOUS RECIPES, neither of which contains more than 5 g of fat, using vegetables and herbs chosen for medicinal properties as well as for their flavour. The Spicy Autumn Pumpkin Soup (see page 90) also boosts winter vitality, its spices helping to sweat out a threatening cold or flu. They can be made and kept for a couple of days, to allow their flavours to develop. Either could be served hot or cold, as the weather dictates. 🍎 SERVINGS ARE FOR TWO PEOPLE, BUT ALL ARE SUITABLE FOR ENTERTAINING; just multiply the quantities accordingly. Remember to work your magic thoughts while you stir your 'cauldron'.

Red pepper and spicy tomato soup

🍎 SERVED WITH BREAD, this makes a lunch that is very low in calories, high in energy and low in fat, or it could make a colourful and warming starter for a posh dinner. When choosing the herbs, remember that parsley is calming for the stomach, whereas fresh thyme is best if you're fighting off a cold.

YOU WILL NEED

1 large red pepper, halved and deseeded 🍎 ½ teaspoon olive oil 🍎 1 small onion, finely chopped 🍎 1 small chilli, deseeded and chopped 🍎 200 ml/7 fl oz tomato juice 🍎 500 ml/18 fl oz chicken or vegetable stock (or a stock cube crumbled in the same quantity of water) 🍎 1 teaspoon sugar 🍎 2 tablespoons plain yoghurt 🍎 sprinkling of chopped fresh parsley or thyme 🍎 damper (see page 89) or other bread, to serve

SERVES 2

🍎 GRILL THE PEPPER HALVES SKIN SIDES UP UNDER A HIGH HEAT UNTIL THE SKIN BLISTERS, then peel away the charred skin and chop the flesh. 🍎 HEAT THE OIL IN A SAUCEPAN, add the onion, chilli and chopped grilled pepper together and cook with the lid on until soft. Add the tomato juice and stock, stirring until well combined. Simmer gently with the lid on for about 20 minutes. Stir in the sugar. 🍎 PULSE IN A BLENDER OR PROCESSOR TO A COARSE PURÉE, KEEPING SOME CONSISTENCY. Pour into warmed bowls and top with a spoonful of yoghurt and a sprinkling of herbs.

Vichyssoise of courgettes, leek and potato

In this aesthetically pleasing dish, two soups are made simultaneously and marbled together when served. This makes it an ideal choice for entertaining. Leek and garlic are renowned gypsy prophylactics against colds.

You will need

For the leek and potato soup: *½ leek, sliced* ● *potato, chopped* ● *250 ml/9 fl oz vegetable stock (or a stock cube crumbled in the same quantity of water)* ● *1 bay leaf* ● *2 teaspoons chopped fresh marjoram* ● *ground black pepper* ● *1 small tub of plain yoghurt*

For the courgette soup: *1 small onion, finely chopped* ● *2 garlic cloves, crushed* ● *3 small courgettes, finely chopped* ● *100 ml/3½ fl oz vegetable stock (or a stock cube crumbled with the same quantity of water)*

To serve: *1 tablespoon chopped fresh coriander or tarragon leaves* ● *pitta bread*

Serves 2

● To make the leek and potato soup: combine the leek, potato, stock, herbs and pepper in a pan. Bring to the boil, cover and simmer for about 20 minutes. Remove the bay leaf and allow to cool slightly. Process with the yoghurt.

● While the leek and potato soup cooks, make the courgette soup: combine the onion, garlic and courgettes with the stock in another pan. Bring to the boil, cover and simmer for 20 minutes. Allow to cool a little, then process as for the leek and potato soup. ● Put each soup into a separate warmed jug and pour into serving bowls from opposite sides. Use a fork to swirl through a simple marble pattern, then serve at once with a garnish of coriander or tarragon, and some pitta bread.

Pasta pisanelli

How could we dedicate a chapter of food to healthy eating without including pasta? This complex carbohydrate is one of the best foods to eat – summer or winter. Only creamy sauces push up the calories, and there are so many wonderful vegetable alternatives. My grandmother used to make this fresh from her garden, but in winter or in the city we are not so lucky. Nevertheless, frozen peas are sweet and retain all the brilliant vitamins and minerals that make this sweet vegetable an unexpected source of good health. In magic, the pea is a symbol of protected love and close affinity, and they are delicious with pasta. Add in or leave out the pancetta or bacon, according to your herbivorous or carnivorous preferences.

YOU WILL NEED

600 g/1¼ lb dried pasta, in any shape you like • *2 tablespoons olive oil* • *2 onions, thinly sliced* • *100 g/3½ oz pine nuts* • *leaves from a sprig of rosemary* • *4 slices of pancetta or bacon, finely chopped (optional)* • *350 g/12 oz frozen or fresh shelled peas* • *350 g/12 oz mange tout (or sugar snap peas)* • *salt* • *2 tablespoons single cream (optional)* • *grated Parmesan cheese, to serve*

SERVES 6

Bring a large pan of water to the boil and, when boiling fast, add salt and throw in the pasta. Stir thoroughly and again every few minutes until cooked. Meanwhile, heat the oil in a pan, add the onions, pine nuts, rosemary and pancetta or bacon (if you are using it) and sauté for a few minutes. Add the peas, put a tight-fitting lid on the pan and steam in the juices until they are tender (usually 4-5 minutes, depending on size, and whether they are fresh or frozen). After a couple of minutes add the mange tout. Keep warm until the pasta is cooked. Drain the pasta, toss with the other ingredients (if you are not watching your calories, add a couple of tablespoons of single cream). Let each person add their own sprinkling of Parmesan cheese.

Cheese and herb fondue

● Perhaps, like my editor, you'll question the wisdom of putting a cheesy-rich dish at the heart of this detox chapter. For me, however, fondue is the centre of my Yule entertaining, honouring as it does the flame at the hearth symbolised under the pot. It can also be a very light meal, and brilliantly social, since everyone literally has to rub shoulders to eat. Simply put plenty of herbs into your fondue to counter some of the richness, and serve with a good salad: winter bliss as it warms your heart and insides. The kirsch also takes on any cold silly enough to take up residence in your body.

You will need

1 garlic clove ● *½ bottle dry white wine* ● *a squeeze of lemon juice* ● *250 g/9 oz Gruyère cheese, grated* ● *250 g/9 oz Emmenthal or Jarlsberg cheese, grated* ● *2 tablespoons kirsch* ● *1 tablespoon cornflour* ● *a pinch of freshly grated nutmeg* ● *a pinch of cayenne pepper* ● *1 tablespoon of fresh chopped herbs, such as oregano, basil, rosemary or coriander* ● *salt and pepper* ● *French bread, chopped roughly into bite-sized chunks, to serve*

Serves 6

● Rub the inside of the fondue pot with the peeled garlic clove. Add the white wine and lemon juice (this adds a little necessary extra acidity) and heat until very hot but not boiling. Then, little by little, start adding handfuls of each cheese and stirring well between additions (use a figure-of-eight motion to help the cheese dissolve). Keep an eye on the heat so as not to burn the cheese. ● When the mixture starts to bubble, combine the kirsch and cornflour and add to the cheese, still stirring. Cook for a couple of minutes until thick, then add the spices, herbs and seasoning to taste. ● Carry to the table with the burner already lit. Encourage all your guests to stir the pot regularly while dipping their bread on the fondue forks and coating with the cheese. If anyone drops their bread into the mixture, they must kiss everyone in the room – pure magic.

Lavender panna cottas with rosewater syrup ❧

DESPITE ALL THOSE GOOD INTENTIONS TO CLEANSE AND DETOX THE SYSTEM, A LIGHT PUDDING IS STILL ALLOWED FROM TIME TO TIME TO REVIVE THE SPIRITS. This particular one is a joy, because it is made the day before, tastes wonderfully subtle and is surprisingly light to eat. ❧ THE SWEET SYRUP WOULD MARK THE END OF ANY ATTEMPTS TO SLIM – but combined with the delicate lavender panna cottas it tastes divine.

YOU WILL NEED

FOR THE PANNA COTTAS: *about 15 lavender stems* ❧ *115 g/4 oz caster sugar* ❧ *500 ml/18 fl oz whole milk* ❧ *4 tablespoons of gelatine* ❧ *5 egg yolks* ❧ *500 ml/18 fl oz double cream* ❧ *rose petals, to decorate*

FOR THE ROSEWATER SYRUP: *450 g/1 lb caster sugar* ❧ *a few drops of rosewater* ❧ *250 ml/9 fl oz water*

SERVES 6

❧ STORE THE LAVENDER FOR A FEW DAYS IN A LITTLE CASTER SUGAR BEFOREHAND, BOTH TO SCENT THE SUGAR AND TO PRESERVE THE LAVENDER. Line 6 heart-shaped moulds with muslin (the muslin needs to over-fill the mould sufficiently to allow the loose ends to wrap over the top of the panna cottas). ❧ NOW STEEP THE SUGAR, MILK AND LAVENDER TOGETHER IN A SAUCEPAN OVER LOW HEAT UNTIL IT GRADUALLY COMES TO THE BOIL. Strain the warm milk mixture through muslin and let it drip through on to the gelatine. Whisk this well to dissolve the gelatine, then whisk in the egg yolks. Chill until the mixture begins to set. ❧ WHIP THE CREAM UNTIL THICK, THEN FOLD GENTLY INTO THE MIXTURE. Pour into the moulds and wrap the loose ends over the top of the panna cottas. Cover with cling film and refrigerate overnight.

❧ ABOUT HALF AN HOUR BEFORE SERVING, MAKE THE SYRUP. ❧ PUT THE CASTER SUGAR AND ROSEWATER INTO A SAUCEPAN WITH THE WATER AND PLACE OVER MEDIUM HEAT. Bring to the boil and simmer for a few minutes, until the mixture forms a syrup. Leave to cool. ❧ LIFT EACH PANNA COTTA OUT OF ITS MOULD WITH THE MUSLIN TAILS, place on individual plates and unwrap the ends of the muslin, leaving the rest in place underneath the heart shape. Pour over the rosewater syrup and dust with a few rose petals.

SUCCESS
IT'S A WRAP

The Menu (serves 6) ❧ Scallops in rice paper rolls

❧ Seafood pancake parcels ❧ Orange-scented lobster

ravioli ❧ Chocolate fondue ❧ Edible spells in brandy

snap wrappers

We arrive at the moment of the stirring earth: the eve of spring. We have come almost

full circle, and our own impulses are towards regeneration and awakening ideas.

In deference to our need to stay wrapped up warm, but to peep out and engage once

again with the natural world, our food has a wrapped theme, which nicely epitomises

the 'wrap' of the old year before true spring emerges

next month. We recall the wrapped pancakes

of Shrove Tuesday, the wrapped rolls and

cookies of Chinese New Year, the

wrapped Valentine's gifts imbued with

love, and the crocus, symbol of the

season, warmly wrapping its treasure,

the precious saffron stamens.

The gentle colours of early spring

● THIS IS THE SEASON THAT WITCHES AND DRUIDS CALL IMBOLC, WHICH TRANSLATED IN THE CHRISTIAN TRADITION TO CANDLEMAS, THE FESTIVAL OF EARLY LIGHTS. Other customs recognise this moment of festival too: Groundhog Day seems to coincide with Imbolc (1st/2nd February), and Chinese New Year falls close to this time. Just after Imbolc, we celebrate Valentine's Day – which has as its precedent the time when the birds choose their mates for the year. We gradually become aware that there are signs of life, the first release from winter slumber, a moment to revive our tired spirits, and to note our progress. ● THE FEASTING THEME IS ONE OF SUCCESS – let's focus our ideas on a lunch or supper to celebrate the completion of the yearly cycle, the gaining of wisdom, the release from dark days. We'll take our cue from the colours of snowdrops, crocuses and other early spring flowers –winter whites, yellows and mauves – and continue the wrapped theme in our decorations. Wrap chairs and drape the dining table in white sheets and dust with glitter to resemble snow and ice. Wrap the plates and tie the cutlery with yellow-gold string or ribbons. Give your guests little wrapped gifts to open. ● THE MAGIC IN THE FOOD CONCERNS SUCCESS AFTER ENDURANCE – the reward after sticking to a long plan or goal. As always, the recipes are designed to form a menu, but if too many wrapped dishes are not to your taste, serve separately or mix and match with dishes from other chapters.

Scallops in rice paper rolls ● THESE LIGHT ROLLS CAN BE SERVED WITH

DRINKS OR AS A STARTER. They're a bit fiddly to make, but provide a wonderful lift to the spirits. ● RICE PAPERS AND TERYAKI SAUCE ARE AVAILABLE FROM ORIENTAL FOOD STORES.

YOU WILL NEED

2 small red chillies, deseeded and chopped ● *2 small green chillies, deseeded and chopped* ● *1 stalk of fresh lemon grass, sliced* ● *2 garlic cloves, peeled* ● *a small piece of fresh ginger, peeled and chopped* ● *a bunch of fresh coriander, finely chopped* ● *125 g/4½ oz creamed coconut* ● *1 teaspoon raw sugar* ● *1 tablespoon teriyaki sauce* ● *squeeze of fresh lime juice* ● *2-3 kaffir lime leaves, cut into strips* ● *200 g/7 oz scallops (shelled weight, but if available, ask for the shells to serve), cut in quarters* ● *200 g/7 oz raw tiger prawns, shelled and cut in half* ● *2 spring onions or shallots, very thinly sliced* ● *12 rice paper wraps* ● *a few fresh mint, coriander or basil leaves or chopped chives*

● PROCESS THE CHILLIES, LEMON GRASS, GARLIC, GINGER AND CORIANDER TO A PASTE. ● IN A WOK OR FRYING PAN, MELT THE CREAMED COCONUT OVER LOW HEAT UNTIL IT IS A THICK LIQUID, BUT NOT OILY. Add in the chilli paste and cook for a few minutes, then add the sugar, teriyaki sauce, lime juice and lime leaves. Cook, stirring, until well combined and fragrant. ● ADD THE SCALLOP AND PRAWN PIECES WITH THE SPRING ONIONS OR SHALLOTS AND TOSS TOGETHER LIGHTLY THROUGH THE PASTE FOR A MINUTE UNTIL JUST COOKED. Remove at once from the heat and set aside to cool. ● WORKING A FEW AT A TIME, BRUSH THE RICE PAPERS WITH A LITTLE WATER UNTIL SOFT, THEN PLACE A SPOONFUL OF THE SCALLOP AND PRAWN MIXTURE ON THE EDGE OF EACH RICE PAPER. Roll up to make a little scroll, folding in the edges as you work, and adding a few leaves of fresh herbs as you go until you have a little parcel with the leaves protruding. Lay them with the join downwards while you make the remaining wraps, then cover them all with a damp tea-towel until you are ready to serve them. ● THEY SHOULD BE SERVED QUITE SOON, so they don't dry out, on a scallop shell, if possible.

Seafood pancake parcels · PERFECT SAVOURY PANCAKES FOR SHROVE TUESDAY.

YOU WILL NEED

60 g/2 oz rice flour · 60 g/2 oz plain flour · 2 eggs · 250 ml/9 fl oz milk · 1 tablespoon olive oil, plus more for frying · a pinch of salt · 100 g/3½ oz fresh crab meat · 100 g/3½ oz fresh lobster meat · 6 large peeled cooked prawns · 15 g/½ oz butter · 2 garlic cloves, chopped · 1 small onion, chopped · 3 tablespoons double cream · 6 spring onions, briefly blanched · a few fresh flowers (orange blossom would be perfect) to garnish

· PUT THE FLOURS, EGGS, MILK, OIL AND SALT IN A FOOD PROCESSOR AND COMBINE THOROUGHLY. Leave this batter to stand for about 20 minutes. · HEAT A PANCAKE OR NON-STICK FRYING PAN, ADD A DROP OF OIL AND TILT THE PAN TO RUN THE OIL ALL AROUND THE BASE AND EDGE OF THE PAN. When really hot but not smoking, pour in just enough batter to make a thin pancake, about 15 cm/6 inches in diameter. Cook over moderate heat until golden on the underside, lifting the edges with a slide so as to avoid sticking, then flip or turn with a spatula and cook the other side. It only takes a minute. Slide the pancake out onto a plate and cook the remaining batter in the same way, putting in a drop of oil each time and watching the temperature of your pan. Layer the pancakes in a pile with sheets of kitchen paper and keep warm. · ROUGHLY CHOP YOUR SEAFOOD. Melt the butter in a pan, add the finely chopped garlic and onion, and cook until just soft. Add the seafood and sauté gently for a few minutes. Add the cream and cook a further minute, then remove. Allow to cool a little. · PLACE A GOOD HEAPED SPOONFUL OF SEAFOOD MIXTURE INTO THE MIDDLE OF EACH PANCAKE. Gather up the edges until you have a little 'bag', and secure them by tying with the long green stems of the blanched spring onions. · SERVE WARM WITH ORANGE CREAM SAUCE (SEE PAGE 133) AND STREW WITH FLOWERS.

The magical art of making pasta ● For me, making and

cooking pasta is the ultimate way to make magic in cookery. My Italian aunt Giovanna used to make this fresh pasta, and I watched her with hungry eyes when I was a child. Yes, it is a labour of love to make your own when there is so much wonderful fresh pasta on offer commercially, but if you wish to weave some special magic, roll up your sleeves one lazy Sunday and discover how thoroughly to bewitch anyone who eats at your table. Essential accompaniments are some Italian opera and a full heart.

Home-made egg pasta dough ● This is a basic recipe for fresh

egg pasta dough, from which you can cut many shapes. You don't need a machine unless you are going to make it often; otherwise, extra time and a sharp knife will do the job. If you don't need such a large quantity use half and freeze the rest.

You will need

450 g/1 lb unbleached flour, plus more for dusting ● *5 large free-range eggs* ● *a tiny pinch of salt*

Serves about 8 as a starter, and 6 generously as a main course

● Put the flour in a large mound on a big bread or pasta board. Make a well in the centre of the flour and place the eggs and salt in the well. Using a large strong fork, very gradually mix the eggs and salt within the well and then, again very gradually and working from the inner circle outwards, incorporate the flour. ● Start pinching and kneading the dough with your floured hands and, working unhurriedly, you will soon get a very elastic dough ball. Knead until all the flour is incorporated into your elastic dough, preferably by hand, or using the special rollers of a pasta machine if you want to use one. If you work it by hand, you will need to use your whole upper torso, and it takes a good quarter of an hour. Allow the dough to rest for about 20-30 minutes, wrapped in cling film. ● The third phase, after mixing and kneading, is stretching. This can be done with a pasta machine or a plain rolling pin, working gently on a freshly floured surface, and stretching the dough out to the thickness you require. For tagliatelle or a little ravioli shape, 2 mm/$^{1}/_{12}$ inch is about right; for other shapes (like lasagne sheets, or noodles for broths), it can be about 3-4 mm/$^{1}/_{8}$-$^{1}/_{6}$ inch.

Cutting and filling pasta ❦ CUTTING THE SHAPE OF PASTA YOU PREFER IS

EASY WITH A SHARP KNIFE, OR YOU CAN USE A PASTRY WHEEL IF YOU WANT SOMETHING MORE ELABORATE. For tagliatelle fold the dough up into a Swiss roll shape and then cut this across into strands which should be about 6 mm/¼ inch wide. If you are opting for ravioli shapes, use the pastry wheel to give you a 'pinked' effect, and make little regular squares that can be folded over to make simple triangles or sandwiched together over a little filling to make a proper pillow of ravioli. (You will only require a teaspoon of stuffing – a little wilted spinach and some ricotta cheese with seasoning and garlic is simple and delicious.)   ❦ LET THE PASTA REST AGAIN, FOR AN HOUR OR SO, WHILE YOU MAKE YOUR SAUCE.

Cooking pasta ❦ WHEN COOKING PASTA, YOU CAN NEVER HAVE TOO MUCH WATER, SO FILL

A LARGE PAN WITH COLD WATER AND BRING IT TO THE BOIL. Add a teaspoonful of salt to the water. Allow 100 g/4 oz pasta per person, drop into the boiling water and stir well. Fresh will take only 1-2 minutes to cook, while the dried varieties take 8-10 minutes. Make sure your choice of sauce is ready by the time the pasta is cooked.

Orange-scented lobster ravioli 🍎 I admit that this dish does

take a little time and trouble. But if you have been game and turned your hand to making your own pasta, you will find the technique gets easier with practice, and this luxurious lobster ravioli is the perfect expression of your new-found culinary skill. If you absolutely can't face making your own pasta, you could use won ton wrappers instead (available from oriental stores). 🍎 The orange that gives this dish its scented flavour was once a fruit of great luxury, and its perfume is calming. Give yourself plenty of time to prepare the ravioli and serve just with a simple salad.

You will need

For the ravioli: *125 g/4½ oz ricotta cheese* 🍎 *1 teaspoon chopped flat-leaf parsley* 🍎 *grated zest of ½ orange, plus a good squeeze of juice* 🍎 *250 g/9 oz cooked lobster meat* 🍎 *white of 1 egg, beaten* 🍎 *600 g/1¼ lb home-made egg pasta dough (see page 132)*

For the Orange Cream Sauce: *300 ml/½ pint double cream* 🍎 *2 tablespoons orange flower water* 🍎 *dash of Cointreau* 🍎 *grated zest of ½ orange*

🍎 First make the filling: in a large bowl mix together the ricotta cheese, parsley, the orange zest plus the juice, and stir well until the ingredients combine. Cut the lobster meat into smallish pieces still big enough to retain its consistency, and add this in, together with about half the egg white, until the mixture holds together nicely. Cover and chill in the refrigerator. 🍎 Meanwhile, roll out your pasta dough to a thickness of about 3 mm/⅛ inch, and use a ravioli cutter (with 'pinked' edges) to cut out squares about 6 x 6 cm/2½ x 2½ inches. Place a teaspoon of the lobster mixture into the middle of each square, then simply fold the pasta along the diagonal to make easy triangles. If the pasta has dried out a little, brush the edge with a tiny brush dipped in the remaining egg white to seal it, using finger pressure to complete. Put the ravioli in the refrigerator again while you make the sauce. 🍎 Gently heat the cream with the orange flower water, Cointreau and the orange zest. Warm through, but remove from the heat at the first bubble. 🍎 Bring a large pan of salted water to the boil and carefully put in the ravioli, one at a time with a slotted spoon. They will cook in 2-3 minutes. Lift out individually with the slotted spoon and place to drain on kitchen towel. Transfer to a bowl and carefully fold over the Orange Cream Sauce.

Chocolate fondue

🍎 THIS IS MY FAVOURITE PUDDING. For me, the joy lies in the expectant looks on the faces of children and adults, who become wonderfully childlike when they see this heading for the table with a candle burner underneath. It is also remarkably easy to make. In this instance, it's the chocolate doing the 'wrapping' of the accompanying morsels of fruit or ice-cream. Heaven on a stick. 🍎 MANY VARIETIES OF FRUIT WORK WELL, but it is particularly delicious with clementine, mandarin or orange segments to carry the flavour right through the meal, or it is wonderful with hulled and halved strawberries. Put your fruit in the refrigerator to chill it for at least an hour, so that the chocolate coats straight on to it when it is dipped. 🍎 THE ULTIMATE EXPERIENCE IS COMBINING THE FONDUE WITH YOUR OWN ICE-CREAM, made a day or two before, especially saffron ice cream, which honours the season and the goddess (see page 38). Cut slices straight from the refrigerator into your guests' dessert dishes, then have them cut off little pieces, put them on their fondue fork, and very quickly dip them in and out of the chocolate. Bliss. Make a wish.

YOU WILL NEED

250 g/9 oz dark chocolate 🍎 *250 ml/9 fl oz double cream* 🍎 *1 tablespoon kirsch or brandy* 🍎 *55 g/1¾ oz chopped almonds or hazelnuts (optional)* 🍎 *chilled mandarin or orange segments or hulled and halved strawberries, to serve*

🍎 BREAK UP THE CHOCOLATE AND MELT IN THE MICROWAVE COOKER ON LOW, checking between each brief burst (or do it in a bain-marie or bowl set over hot water). Stir in the cream until completely incorporated, followed by the alcohol and the nuts if you are using them. Carry the bowl straight to the flame to keep it molten.

Edible spells in brandy snap wrappers ● These are

AN OLD-FASHIONED FAVOURITE, AND IT IS FUN TO SEE THEM MADE INTO LITTLE SPELLS FOR GOOD LUCK AND SUCCESS — like fortune cookies. You need the left-over rice paper from the starter course.

You will need

90 g/3¼ oz butter, plus more for greasing the baking sheets ● *3 tablespoons golden syrup* ● *60 g/2 oz lightly packed brown sugar* ● *35 g/1¼ oz plain flour* ● *1 teaspoon ground ginger*

To fill and decorate: *24 edible rice papers* ● *food colouring of your choice* ● *whipped cream*

Makes about 24

● Preheat the oven to 190°C/375°F/Gas 5 and grease several baking sheets well with butter. ● Put the butter, syrup and sugar in a saucepan and stir over low heat until melted and combined. Remove from the heat and sift in the flour and ginger together. Mix well. ● Put teaspoonfuls of the mixture well spaced (caution — they spread: try just 2-3 per sheet) on well-greased baking sheets. Bake, in batches if necessary, in the oven for 5 minutes, then remove and allow to cool on the tray for 1 minute. ● Use a spatula to lift them off the tray and, while they are still warm and pliable, roll them around the clean handle of a wooden spoon (you will need several spoons on the go to allow them to cool on the handle itself). Remove carefully from the spoon. ● Write little spells for love and success on the rice paper: use food colouring and either a clean nib pen or a fine paint brush. (You will find short, appropriate spells in my other books: *Hocus Pocus, Bewitched, Enchanted, Wishing Spells* or *White Magic*.) Make the little spells into scroll shapes, push them through a brandy snap, add some piped cream and tie with a ribbon around the whole biscuit. Everything but the ribbon can then be eaten.

The witch's herbal ● A guide to the magical properties of herbs and spices

● Here is an overview of some of the most popular, accessible or interesting herbs, flowers and spices for use in your cookery. Find ways to incorporate them into your everyday recipes, or spice up old favourites. ● In the twenty-first century, when supermarket salad leaves are now more exciting and varied than ever, it hardly seems necessary to describe the need for a varied herbal diet to maintain health and add interest to your cooking. However, our ancestors had little access to such a wealth of natural vitamins, and a diet enriched with herbs and herbal tonics was often the difference between sickness and health. Advice on this subject was perhaps the most valuable a witch could give, and added the dimension of magic in the everyday and banal. ● Some of the following herbs formed the nucleus of the witch's garden, and were prescribed for health and their other magical properties. Herbs that help to keep you calm, for instance, must allay many problems before they arise. If you vary your diet to include many of these delicate but powerful ingredients on a regular basis, you will surely maintain strength and good spirits and rarely be on the sick list, as well as creating magical effects for those who eat with you.

● It should be easy to buy many of them potted fresh, or flat-packed at the supermarket, but if you have a little space, grow them yourself on a windowsill or balcony for the added pleasure and benefits of nurturing a living plant. ●

Why not fill a large salad bowl with as many herby leaves and flowers from this list as you can manage, spreading magic and mystery – as well as health – among your friends and family. Prepare a light lunch for a friend who is down or has a few problems, and talk about things together over the meal. The release of problems is vital to daily well-being, for problems hung onto are the cause of many ultimately serious health problems. ● Or, make compresses, and muslin herb-bags for use in the bath, when the spirits are under attack, drawing information and inspiration from these herbs. Choose an appropriate moment to boost your psychological and physical self-heal before things get out of hand, or just before a big evening of entertaining. Always take time for yourself.

Herbs and flowers

(APOTHECARY'S) ROSE: Forever associated with life and love, the truth is that the *Rosa gallica* has a myriad uses: it is delicious added to ordinary foods to improve their appeal to the senses, the mind and the body. Cakes, jams and ice-creams, sweets, wines and salads will all gain from the addition of rose petals (remove the white bit at the base of the petal, which has a slightly bitter taste); crushed petals – and, of course, the hips in autumn – form the basis of a well-known syrup for coughs and chest complaints, and a decoction made by adding plenty of rose petals to about 1 litre of boiling water and infusing for ten minutes will make an excellent tonic for the old and young. It is also useful for anyone who has just finished a course of antibiotics, as it re-establishes the intestinal flora. And, of course, it will always cheer the spirits to see roses added to anything.

BASIL: The culinary herb needs no-one to argue its case. It has many valued properties – not least that basil tea is very effective in settling bad nerves, and, it is also known to stimulate the brain to work effectively. This makes it an ideal choice for anyone facing exams or other work stress. Wine which has basil leaves steeped in it is an effective tonic and – almost certainly – has some aphrodisiac effects. Basil is a herb connected with love spells and potions. Soups, stews, pasta dishes, vegetable recipes and salads will all gain immensely from the addition of a few loosely torn basil leaves: fresh is essential.

CALENDULA: This lovely herb, whose petals look delightful in salads or soups, reduces fevers, soothes intestinal disorders, is antiseptic and antifungal, and helps to heal skin problems. It is also used as a rinse for the hair, to lighten it. My grandmother swore by it as a light tea to ease period pain and PMT and to regularise the cycle altogether – but she also said it made you flirtatious. You've been warned!

CARAWAY: A crucial ingredient for flavouring breads, the seeds have properties similar to fennel and dill, but are also anti-spasmodic and thus a good overall health tonic. You can add the young shoots of caraway to salads to sweeten the breath and relieve heartburn.

CHERVIL: Valued since the Middle Ages for medicinal properties and as a love amulet, this delicate herb is diuretic, cleanses the liver and kidneys, and was used to bathe women after they had given birth – possibly because of its reputation for dissolving blood clots. Today it is added to salads, and is also delicious added to scrambed eggs; the leaves add flavour and are a good general tonic.

CORIANDER: A stimulant herb, it was prized as an aphrodisiac and believed to combat fatigue and apathy. The Chinese feel it bestows immortality. Interestingly, the seeds have a mildly narcotic effect and are sedative, ease headache, tension and nervous exhaustion. If you're lucky they may also make you feel frisky!

DANDELION: An essential in any of grandmother's salads, young dandelion leaves were also added to wine and the root made into a coffee substitute. A thoroughly beneficial herb, add it to your diet in any way – to eat or drink – and it will flush the kidneys, help liver complaints, purify the blood, aid digestion, act as a mild laxative, tonic, improve appetite, and probably relieve symptoms of rheumatism and arthritis. The expressed sap was a valued treatment for warts. But if you drink dandelion coffee late at night you may understand the reason for its French nick-name, *pissenlit*, so be careful!

Garlic: If you don't find this bulb unpleasant, let it form the basis of a healthy diet. A powerful antiseptic and antibiotic, garlic is a brilliant general tonic, promotes appetite, can be used to treat diarrhoea, nausea and stomach cramp, is good for the circulatory system (and therefore, heart), relieves cold and flu symptoms, and, of course, keeps vampires away! Along with onions, it reduces blood pressure, aids digestion, eliminates toxins from the system, and regulates all the vital organs, including blood sugar levels. Use fresh bulbs, as prolonged storage reduces the impact of the plant. If the smell really offends you, try chewing copious quantities of parsley to counteract it. Green garlic, called for in some recipes, is the very young, soft, fresh-picked bulb which has a subtle taste, rather than the powerful (and to some, offensive) smell of the usual dried garlic bulb.

Lavender: The medicinal properties long ascribed to lavender have now been backed up by modern research. This sedative, tranquillising herb has been used for centuries to counter insomnia, headaches, nervous stress, fever, flu and other respiratory disorders, and externally to treat burns and bacterial skin problems. Nowadays the oil replaces the need for strong decoctions, and just a drop used neat on a burn, bite or area of rough skin will speed healing and ease the pain. The flavour is inspirational in cakes, jellies, ice-cream, as well as in fish or chicken dishes. For some reason its scent releases a feel-good factor in our brains, and it may even aid in cell renewal. A must for the senses as well as the first aid box.

Lemon Balm: Paracelsus, the Greek father of medicine, deemed it the reviver of the spirits, and this wonderful herb is an essential in the witch's store cupboard. Its sedative properties make it a good ingredient in herb pillows, but the anti-spasmodic properties make it a de-stressing herb ideal for women who are tense and nervy. In fact, it is highly regarded as a gentle aphrodisiac as it calms the nerves and lifts the spirits. The leaves are wonderful added to sandwiches and salads, omelettes, or fish dishes; it also adds a tangy lemon flavour to sweets and cakes. It is an ideal general tonic and is easily grown in a pot, even throughout winter. Make a tea for the end of your meal, infusing 30 g fresh leaves in 500 ml boiled water for 5 minutes, then sweeten with honey. It is said to promote long life and happiness (and make your partner frisky!).

Marjoram (or Oregano): A herb with strong sedative properties, so it must be taken cautiously; however, mild teas certainly aid restfulness. This herb symbolised happiness to the Greeks and Romans, so it was regarded as lucky for lovers. My grandmother respected this herb for its ability to relieve hay fever – which she did by saturating cotton wool in a strong solution and inhaling it. This can also be an effective treatment for headaches. My own discovery concerning this herb is its powerful capacity to heal blistered feet…

Mint: cooking with mint will naturally freshen your breath, counter mouth complaints, and calm the nerves. An ideal choice of tea after meals, mint settles the stomach and also helps to neutralise headaches caused by tiredness and nausea. It was thought to bolster one's inclination for love-making, too. It is very easy to grow in your kitchen window.

Nasturtium: Leaves, seeds and flowers are all valued for their tonic effects. Add the leaves and flowers to sandwiches for a lovely peppery taste, similar to cress, and discover whether they have a positive effect on your skin, hair, nails and eyes. They also lift your mood by their colour and prettiness in food. The seeds make a natural antibiotic, so they are useful for countering food poisoning or the onset of colds and flu.

Like watercress, a strong tonic made from flowers, leaves and seeds will nourish the hair follicles, making you feel and look beautiful as well as bouncy.

PARSLEY: This common but underused herb has legendary powers to counter the strong smells of garlic and onions, freshens the breath, disguises drinking, and is said to be an aphrodisiac. On a less exotic note, it aids digestion, eases flatulence, and with a high vitamin C and iron content is a good tonic and additive to salads. Do not take when pregnant.

ROSEMARY: The most famous ingredient of Hungary Water, which was considered an elixir of youth. Rosemary is certainly a cardio-tonic, stimulant herb which works as antiseptic, diuretic and anti-spasmodic. It is added to wine for flavour and, it is believed, bestows prosperity if you toast the gods with it. A mild infusion (like a light tea) made from flowering tips and leaves, will make a good tonic for convalescents and anyone suffering from depression or anxiety. Rosemary also seems to have a stimulating effect on the brain and memory recall – so no excuses for anyone to forget your phone number after dinner! Symbolic of the gift of friendship, a pot of rosemary is traditional to give to a friend moving into a new home.

SAGE: There is an old proverb which runs 'Why should a man die, who has sage in his garden?' A tradition from medieval times suggested that sage in the garden, and consumed regularly in the diet, ensured prosperity in the household. Sage tea sweetened with honey is wonderfully soothing for sore throats.

TARRAGON: The best cure for hiccups that I know. Beloved of cooks for its culinary dexterity, the original popularity of this herb was its capacity once again to aid in digestion and soothe pain – especially toothache. Tear the leaves and scatter them over chicken and fish dishes at the last minute to keep the properties of the herb in peak form.

THYME: My mother and father's favourite herb, perhaps. This wonderful little spirit is Nature's own antibiotic. A cold picked up early can be nipped in the bud by adding fresh thyme leaves to food or making a strong tea from the plant. Use the oil, diluted of course, to make a therapeutic rub for a stimulating massage, and in the treatment of muscular aches and pains and sciatica; also to bathe in to counter depression.

VIOLETS: One of my favourites, this sweetly fragrant, fragile-looking flower was beloved of the Greeks and Romans, as well as by Napoleon. And why? It was said to confer fertility, was a requisite in love potions, and made a delicious fragrant wine. Valued to treat headache, migraine, insomnia and nervous tension, violet contains the glycoside of salicylic acid (aspirin again), while the leaves and flowers are delicious to eat and look pretty in foods. Use the flowers in cakes and salads, leaves too, and enjoy the aroma they release as you dine.

WATERCRESS: Easily absorbed into soups, sandwiches and salads, this herb has been used since Roman times in many interesting ways. It was thought to promote appetite, regarded for its aphrodisiac qualities, and could help lower blood-sugar levels. It is also very nutritious, rich in vitamins and minerals – making it a good all-purpose additive to your general diet. Externally, its juice was applied as a tonic for abundant, healthy hair; and it was also valued for improving skin quality.

WILD STRAWBERRY: Used for centuries in love spells, and regarded by generations as a magic plant, scientific research is now able to confirm many of its traditionally regarded properties. Fruits, leaves and seeds can all be used, and have diuretic and antiseptic properties. The fruits are high in iron and potassium, and are nutritious as well as palliative. They soothe the spirits on the metaphysical plane, and chapped and sunburnt skin on a more physical one.

Spices ● YOU KNOW HOW MUCH THEY ADD TO THE SMELL AND TASTE OF YOUR COOKING, but here is a little guide to their additional graces. It is a wise practice to roast seeds first, to kill any bacteria they might have been sprayed with beforehand.

ALLSPICE: This smells like cinnamon and cloves in one, and the smell of the flowers in perfume in the plantations creates an atmosphere of romance. Use the berries to flavour both sweet and savoury foods, or add to warm drinks.

BAY: The leaves are used in *bouquet garni* and add a lovely aroma when cooked, but don't forget the berries and twiggy stems in barbecues and fires. This produces a mildly narcotic effect, inducing a gentle trance and relaxation.

CARDAMOM: A well-deserved reputation for heightening the senses, calming digestion, freshening the breath, and countering fatigue make this an excellent spice to play with in entertaining – especially if you have romance on your mind. It works well in sweets as well as curries and stews, and makes an interesting flavour for Italian home-made ice cream.

CINNAMON: A central ingredient in pot-pourri and pomanders, this wonderful spice needs no introduction. It is a favourite aphrodisiac for gentlemen, and the scent of it in candles, punches and bakery entices the senses to relax and feel happy. Particularly in the bedroom, cinnamon has a seductive but particularly cosy impact.

CLOVE: Deserving its reputation as a room fragrancer, the scent of this lovely spice in cookery is comforting and cheering, and was traditional in mixtures for love. It is tasty added to almost anything – pickles, cold meats, cakes, casseroles and drinks.

CUMIN: A vital component in several spicy mixtures, it is at home in Indian, Thai, Mexican, European and Moroccan cuisine. Whether it is understood as aphrodisiac to all, it is certainly a seductive addition to the *ras el hanout* beloved in Arabic cooking, and can be added to stews, breads and meats very effectively. Remember, the seeds are best roasted to bring out their flavour, and also to kill off any toxins from their growth process.

NUTMEG: Another reputed aphrodisiac, nutmeg makes a headier brew out of alcoholic drinks – so beware an added sense of intoxication. The oil lifts depressed spirits and also helps to improve one's self-image and confidence. It is also a predominantly male aroma (for seduction), and is mildly narcotic – so use only in small measures. Nutmeg is excellent in cakes, sweets, drinks, it is also lovely with vegetables such as carrot, spinach and potato.

PEPPER: Pepper helps to sharpen your guests' appetites – so a peppery starter will put them in the mood for dining. It also aids digestion, and helps reduce tummy problems. Get a good grinder, and offer cracked pepper in various colours.

SAFFRON: The aphrodisiac scent of seduction is saffron, but remember that too much may be narcotic, so use only the pinch that your budget will allow. The delicious flavours come into their own in fish and rice dishes, but experiment with just a hint in cakes, custards and pastries.

STAR ANISE: This has a warm and sexy smell, but the flavour is actually very subtle. It is divine in chicken dishes, rice, and after-dinner drinks. The Latin name translates as 'alluring' – need we say more?

VANILLA: This is the pod from an orchid – so vanilla ice-cream could be called orchid ice-cream. The scent of vanilla in the air in the kitchen adds a topnote of mystery and surprise to the evening ahead. The pods will flavour sugar in an airtight jar (leave one in there), as well as creams, sauces, drinks, and pot pourris. Its aphrodisiac properties deserve serious consideration.

Index

First published in 2001 by
Quadrille Publishing Limited
Alhambra House
27-31 Charing Cross Road
London WC2H 0LS

PUBLISHING DIRECTOR Anne Furniss

DESIGN Jim Smith

COPY EDITOR Lewis Esson

EDITORIAL ASSISTANT Katie Ginn

PRODUCTION Nancy Roberts

© TEXT Titania Hardie 2001
© PHOTOGRAPHS Sara Morris 2001
© LAYOUT AND DESIGN Quadrille
Publishing Limited 2001

British Library Cataloguing
in Publication Data
A catalogue record for this book
is available from the British Library
ISBN 1 903845 13 0

Printed and bound in Germany